JOHN BAILEY

TROUT AT TEN THOUSAND FEET

REFLECTIONS OF A PASSIONATE FISHERMAN

NEW HOLLAND

This edition published in 2008
First published in 2001 by New Holland Publishers (UK) Ltd
London · Cape Town · Sydney · Auckland

2 4 6 8 10 9 7 5 3

Garfield House, 86–88 Edgware Road, London W2 2EA, United Kingdom

80 McKenzie Street, Cape Town 8001, South Africa

Unit 1, 66 Gibbes Street, Chatswood, NSW 2067, Australia

218 Lake Road, Northcote, Auckland, New Zealand

ISBN 978 1 84773 124 1

Publishing Manager: Jo Hemmings
Designer: Anne Wilson
Cover Design: Design Revolution
Cover Artwork: Mark Roberts
Production: Joan Woodroffe

Printed and bound in Malaysia by Times Offset (M) Sdn Bhd

CONTENTS

IN APPRECIATION

Appreciation? Acknowledgements? I'm not sure about these words, I guess accomplices is a far better term. In fact, in sincerity, this book isn't really mine at all but rather the story of countless men and women who've had such an impact on my life for nearly half a century. And the world's best dog of course … but more of him shortly.

In the early days, I can't help believing my parents colluded more than they should have done with my fishing career. And I'll always blame my grandmother for inspiring me with mighty tales of derring-do performed by my late grandfather. On the literary side, Bernard Venables and B.B. have both got a lot to answer for. Their evocative prose carried me away to magical fishing lands when, in reality, I'd got far more important things to do. Or so it seemed to everyone who ever taught me.

In a fundamental, guts of my life way, I'd like to thank Reelscreamer, who has nourished every piscatorial ambition of mine even if he hasn't actually cast a fly on the water himself now for nearly twenty years. I'd like to thank Maddie, a spaniel of enormous angling ability for all my success in Scotland. Truly. And for bringing Christopher along who's a good cook and even better company. Johnny Jensen certainly plays a central role: as you'll see, he's been responsible for many of the messes I've got myself in. Thank you Peter Smith. I guess you'll never know how sane you've kept me over the past fifteen years.

In Scotland, I'd like to thank the Heaths, the Hetts, all the Johns, and the Barbers for frequent shelter given from the storm. Mention must be made of a certain Dutchman who so frequently allowed me use of his most magical estate. Thank you Dennis and thank you Norrie. I'm praying for you.

In Greenland, I'd like to thank Sexy Morten, less sexy Niels, the Swedish pilots who appeared with beer one night, the musk ox that spared me, and Johnny for his impersonation of Basil Fawlty. Thank you Mick and Simon for keeping me laughing for three weeks and Stuart for deciding to pack at three o'clock one morning. Thank you James for slipping off the glacial ice and not knocking your head clean off.

Let's take Russia, Siberia, Kazakhstan and all those far-flung, ruinous states together. Thank you Sasha for saving my life and Mr. Mochanov — wherever you are now — for not thinking it worth taking. Thank you Michael, Uncle and my dear German friend Berdt … but I still think Michelle Pfeiffer is the most beautiful woman in the world, whatever you say. Thank you Niels Ortoft for showing that a three hundred pound fish can be caught on a salmon fly and thank you Pasha for the fact that I'm not lingering now in an Iranian jail. Thank you to Michael for organising a few eastern calamities and to Olav and Christian who made them quite fun. Thank you Georg for cooking lenok trout almost before they'd been landed and Gennardi for showing me your bottom-of-the-garden dunny. Thanks to Brian Pilcher and Keith Musto for providing me with clothing that has saved me from frostbite many times.

In Mongolia, I must thank Petr (two of them in fact), the Mighty Radim and our own Friar Tuck, Jan, even though one of his farts occasioned an earthquake. I'd like to

embrace all the fellow Mongolian travellers — Rob, Phil, Leo, Simon, Ade, Phil, Chris, Ian... you're just too numerous to mention but I love you all. Thank you Gamba for being invariably manic and my Mongolian brother Batsokh for just about everything. Thank you Ennisch for dreams and for the Red Baron for flying me and then crashing me in stomach-churning safety. Frank, we are all thinking of you. Always. And Dave, thanks for lending me that rod for the past five years. Or is it six?!

In India and out-lying lands, I'd like to thank Keith for introducing me to cards and Simon to whisky. I'd like to thank John Edwards for always setting such a fine, well-dressed example and, way back Linda, Dinesh, Peter, Paul, John, George... we only needed Ringo! Joe will have to do instead. A hundred and seven 'thank yous' to the Boys of Nepal and down in the south, Bola and Suban — that was the best month of my life. Thank you Alan for that smile of yours: bigger than the Indian sun.

I'd like to thank the Norfolk wild bunch — Billy T, the beloved man of three halves, Joe, Ching, Bernie Bishop, who rescued me from a life of sprout picking with lascivious women, and Geoff Crowe for showing me how life should be lived.

On Acklins I'd like to thank Roger, my fellow carnival queen and gently calming influence. Thank you Tony, Philip and Magnus especially, for maintaining rigorous standards. Amos, Elvis and Fidel, please don't forget us.

On the Baltic, I'd like to thank Michael for being so gentle and Johnny for catching the biggest fish ever...as usual. Up in North Uist I'd like to thank Maddie for sniffing out the big ones and looking after Christopher. Thank you Christopher for letting me play Perfect Day. Elsewhere around the New World, I'd like to thank Big Bob and brother Wayne, everybody I met in New Zealand because you just can't find more generous people anywhere. The same goes for America but let me especially thank John Hemmingway for taking an interest. For the rest, in no particular order, let me thank Paul for providing both inspirations and warnings, all at Launce Nicholson's tackle shop and Simon whose luck with women and cards is extraordinary. Not that he's ever exploited either, Sally, I promise.

Lest this should seem heavily biased towards the male, let me say that women figure every bit as large. Thank you Sue for constant, 'alluring' advice. Hats off to Shirley for proving what wimps men are. God save Carol for working with me at all hours and trying to stop me worrying and to several hundred cooks doing a brilliant best in impossible kitchens with food you wouldn't even recognise as edible. Thank you to Charlotte for lending me Johnny — I told you I'd bring him back. Thank you Yvonne at New Holland for agreeing that Trout can fly. Thank you, Jo, for believing in it — and me — in the first place and then proving to be the most sensitive editor I've ever known. And thank you, dearest Joy. As you will read, this book is so much about you.

Finally, I would like to thank Mohammed and all the staff at La Roseraie, Morocco for the sanctuary provided to complete what the above gang have given me to say. And apologies to the unmentioned many who have contributed to the wreck of a man I am today.

JOHN
THE
FISH

'I yearned to become a part of that world, to be with those fish, those great olive-backed tench as they sauntered down the avenues amidst the weed, across floors of polished sand, into their darkened rooms beneath the drapes of lilies.'

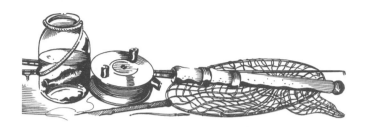

VOICES FROM THAT AUGUST DAY will never be stilled, not now. Voices fine-tuned by fear raking over the marsh. Forty years ago? It seems like an eternal yesterday. My parents tense, sensing the blade of panic cutting the sea wind. My father running towards the desperately waving figures. I followed, like a child does, eager to be in on the action, lagging a couple of paces behind to be on the periphery. Two women and a man standing above the sluices where the river runs to meet the sea. Pointing, shrieking — a rising tide in the agony of men that rips your chest apart. 'My daughter. Oh, my God. My little girl...' A woman's voice, sobbing. My father, a hero in the war, a hero still, strips and in a graceful, diving arc enters the pool. I watch him breasting the currents like a white otter. Amazement and a burst of hope stifling the pain, hold the horror in suspension. My mother comforts the woman. I'm small, shy and I recognise my father as successful, important, his advice sought everywhere. But here, for once, I knew he was wrong. 'My little boy plays in the sink,' said my mother always, teasingly, lovingly and she was right. Almost since crawling, I'd been compelled to learn how water works, how it curls and creates its own world. Now I understood both the river beneath us and that my father was exhausting himself in the wrong place. The river and the tide were

meeting at such a pace that anybody caught between would be lifted, then pushed down and trundled away from the pool. Too diffident to voice my instinctive knowledge, I slipped unnoticed through the reed beds and there, at the first bend, a golden-haired girl lay in the margins, dress rippling, face as though in sleep.

I think I shouted. I'm told I was found in the water with her, pushing her back to the bank but in truth the rest of that day is remote. I seem to remember my father over her, breathing into her. I know she lived and that it was I who became the hero. The little unexpected hero. 'How did you know...?' 'What you did...' 'How can we ever...?' What was important to me though was that never again did my mother laugh when she saw me on the stool by that sink. No longer was I 'an odd little fish'. Henceforth, I was her 'little fish' only, as though my strangeness were now accepted.

In truth, I'd always been aware my obsession had isolated me from the other children who were only interested in cars, trains, dolls or war games in the school yard. That near-tragic day gave me a confidence and eased the nagging doubts I had about my own passions. All I'd ever wanted to do was to see more and more fish, glistening in the water, dancing in the waves, big fish, small fish. Colourful fish or fish that to the rest of the world might well seem drab but to me shone like the sun. Jam-jar fish at first, minnows, sticklebacks and then gudgeon — nobody's favourite fish but mine with those delicate, shifting glints of blue. The dart-like silver of the dace, another baby miracle in a magic world. Perch, beautifully barred. Roach, pearl-like silver. Carp, golden-scale clad. Pike, new-moon toothed and mottled menace. On and on, more and more fish, always seeking to complete a cosmic vision. It wasn't the 'twitcher' mentality obsessively ticking away at a list, it was something more than that and still is. More like a dabbling in wonderment.

Nose pressed to the bowl, watching my two wretched goldfish swim a miserable, circular life, agog at how they twisted, turned, hovered

and fanned those fabulous fins. An old sink outside in the garden, filled with murky water and mysterious fish…the weather loach that only came up before a thunderstorm and wriggled manically at the edges of the porcelain. What went on in that life during the endless months between? What could have been the signals that sparked in its little brain as the thunder began to roll? The baby tench that blew up bubbles every time I dropped in chopped garden worms and the eel that only moved at night, snaking out to engulf the tadpoles I had moved in from the farm pond. A sinister world but enthralling for all that, almost uniquely unknowable.

It was never a case of whether I wanted to go fishing or not, for if I wanted to see different types of fish, it was very often necessary to catch them. And, to be honest, I was compelled towards the sport so inexorably that I believe I'm a fisherman either because of genetics or reincarnation. My grandfather was an angler, quite famous in his day and because he died sixteen years before I was born he obviously didn't influence me directly. Genetically, though, who can tell? And once I was regressed by a throaty, floaty sort of woman enveloped in swirls of hazy purples and only held down to earth by lashings of golden jewellery. When I was in a trance – overcome by eyes, voice and perfume – it emerged that I'd been a Highlander in a past life, during the eighteenth century when I'd gone away to fight and

suffered a hideous death. Don't try telling me there wasn't a stream running through my glen and that I hadn't winkled out a trout or two before going off to tackle the Sassenachs.

The first years of my fishing life were gruelling, any tiny success hard won. They were spent largely on a mean, oil-veneered canal on the outskirts of Manchester. The nasty, sharp grit of the towpath was for ever in my knees or the palms of my hands after I'd fallen from my bike or been in a fight with any one of the innumerable gangs of tough lads that patrolled from one bridge to another. Boys' tackle then was cheap and seemingly designed to frustrate you. Lines 'bird-nested' as if through a hideous black magic. Reels seized when it rained and froze in the snow. A whole cane rod had the delicacy of a yard brush. The winters were achingly miserable, feet frozen in thin Wellington boots whilst the anoraks of those days soaked up sleet like blotting paper. If you ever did hook a fish, chances were it would be as pale, as thin and as sick as the rest of us. The first roach I ever caught turned out to be blind in not one but both eyes, which explains why it overlooked the awkward hook and gangly knot in the first place.

Even then, travel seemed to offer a way out and at a seemingly vast distance from my home lay the Roman Lakes, grubby but full of fish. This Eden, though, could only be reached by a twelve mile round trip, a trek for a six year old. Worse, the path down to the lakes took me past the tramp's cave and I could never be sure whether he'd be there and come out at me in the half darkness as I hared for home. I couldn't know if he wished me harm but he looked grotesque and once he came so close to catching me, I could smell the staleness on his breath. Eventually, the paper reported that the police had found his body but I was never convinced. In fact, the walk home became worse after that because it was his ghost that chased me. I could hear his boots on the dark stones padding relentlessly through the merciless night.

In these early days what I liked most about fishing was reading about it. Bed and books. An apple and milk. Angling adventures far away in space and time. It wasn't too hard to dream of better worlds holding waters with fish more than matchstick big. Endless images, unlimited possibilities. A Hampshire chalk stream running through lush water meadows dotted with willows, a church spire in the distance and a lark overhead. No rough boys there; just huge, speckled trout lazily plopping at mayflies the size of parachutes. And then, as I've already written, my parents did take me away to the sea. Many days they left me at a lake wondrously named Bayfield and possessing the halo of beauty I'd only ever dreamed of before. The toe of the lake almost always lay in wooded shade, even though it was high summer, but when I walked out into the poppy-strewn field, the sun was full glow onto it, lighting it up with glistening brightness. Standing behind some yellow flag irises, I peered in and

for the very first time saw some truly huge fish for myself – real fish, not just drawings – living in another world, a parallel universe so close to mine I felt I could reach out and touch it. I yearned to become a part of that world, to be with those fish, those great olive-backed tench as they sauntered down the avenues amidst the weed, across floors of polished sand, into their darkened rooms beneath the drapes of lilies. I understood that those fish were beyond my powers to catch but that did not matter then and nor have similar failures ever done so since. Just watching them showed me that the world could be kind, that the books that had so long sustained me contained more than dreams but were truth itself. That morning was my defining moment in life, I suppose. You could say either that I've never grown up since or that I was mature then. I'd found my purpose and never once have I been tempted to deviate from it.

Back in Manchester, I tried to explain my discovery to Alan Socket, my closest friend and to Margaret who I'd loved absolutely for all the preceding term. It was all perhaps too heavy for playground banter and neither understood. After a minute or two Brian's eyes glazed over and he went off to play marbles but, then, he wasn't as plugged in as his name might suggest. Margaret, though, did try at break, at lunch and then again on the walk homewards. But, even aged seven, she was woman enough to recognise a loser and pretty enough to realise she could do better.

I suspect my parents had a rather hard time but in return handed out wildly contradictory messages. On Saturday I'd hear that all that matters in life is happiness and it was fine if I became a water bailiff, pedalling my bike along the towpaths of the future. Come Sunday, I'd be told that money doesn't grow on trees and why wasn't I memorising the yard of the Iliad that I'd been set for homework? Nor did they seem pleased when, at the age of twelve, it came to light that I'd been writing fishing articles during the year's maths lessons. That two had been published and had earned me the grand total of four pounds ten shillings (£4.50) didn't seem to make up for the fact that I'd come thirty sixth out of a class of thirty seven. As it was pointed out to me, it was after all the inevitable Master Socket that propped the rest of the class up in everything.

Give and take, revenge is sweet. 'Boy escapes with his life,' ran the local paper's report. I throw out my father's lump hammer the thousandth time that winter of the 1963 freeze. It had to happen, the rope catching my ankle, and I float through the crystal air after the fourteen pounds of unforgiving metal. Cometh the canal, somehow escapeth the boy. Half a frozen mile away lived a friend. His introduction was recorded in the family annals: 'Hello? Did you have a son called John Bailey? Yes? Well, he fell in.'

Ten now and my parents drove me to a remote hotel perched right by the side of a wild and swelling river. They stayed with me for two days to check everything out and then left me for the remainder of the month. Of course, today when no child is allowed a rod's length from a responsible adult, such a decision would be seen as irresponsible, insane and probably criminal but to this very day I thank my parents from the bottom of my heart for it. There were times admittedly I felt very small, when I fell off a bridge, broke a rod, cut my knee and sobbed miserably in the dripping rain. But that was the great thing about a child's life in those days: you simply had to sort it out for yourself without any adult to help you back on your feet. It's my sincerely held belief that both pleasure and pain are more vivid if you experience them for yourself rather than through outside intermediaries. Children, as much as grown ups, need their space to explore the world at first-hand. And how wonderful it can be.

Once more, I fell seriously in love. Together, we went to the cinema at a nearby seaside town to watch John Wayne and Steve McQueen kill their respective Indians and Germans. Her name was Julie and I really feel we would have been together still but for the fact that she was twenty-five years my senior and the hotel manageress. A fellow guest was an artist, and the type of man my father would describe as a bounder, complete with cravat, MG sports car (which he drove wearing leather gloves) and who I suspected of having similar designs on Julie. He was earnest with me about his paintings but, when I pointed out that there were two trees close to a bridge that he was drawing, not one as he'd portrayed it, he became agitated. 'What is reality? Am I real? Are you real? Never forget, young John, we create our own reality.' Hardly surprising I was so convinced that I was the man for Julie.

DIARY ENTRY AUGUST 3RD 1961
'It rained all night in big dollops and this morning the river was dirty and in flud (sic). I caught eight trout (best yet) and saw some salmon. A sheep was in the river but it was dead. I slipped and bashed my knee and Julie said later I was a poorly tomato. She is very nice and I love her but I don't always know why she says things.' (Years later, when I phoned Julie to tell her of the death of my parents she said fondly, 'Still the poor little martyr'. So that was it!)

Shortly after the flood, I saw a salmon bow-wave up river through the tiny village looking like a submarine. Also watching the fish was a much older lad whom I'd heard referred to as Murphy. At a guess, I'd say he was around eighteen, lean and mean so I agreed at once to meet him by the bridge at five p.m. as he commanded. He led the way determinedly down river, way past the point that the hotel fishing finished. With a quick look right and left, he climbed a fence and I scurried in his wake, deep into enclosed woodland.

17

Our pace slackened and he moved slowly from one overhanging tree to the next, peering intently into the water beneath. Then he froze, cupped his hands around his eyes and spent a full minute in quivering concentration. He beckoned me towards him and pointed. A salmon. A silver, splendid salmon. In a trice he'd cut himself a stick, pulled out a snare from his pocket and was inching the glinting copper necklace towards the fish's gills. I had been nervous but now I was enthralled. All I could see was that velvety fish hanging in the crystal water. Which suddenly exploded in front of us. Murphy was in grave danger of being pulled in and yelled at me to anchor him round the waist. We pulled mightily and the salmon yanked back but after a frenzied thirty seconds or so the fish soared skywards like a cork from a bottle and we fell on it, rapturous in the long grass.

When we'd sorted ourselves out, when the quiverings of the silver giant at our feet had ceased, Murphy turned to me and said, 'Take it. It's your fish.' For a moment I could see myself walking into the bar in triumph, the fish over my shoulder, its nose dangling down to my Wellington tops. What would they all say? Wouldn't I be Julie's hero? I'd like to be able to say something dignified about myself at this point. That the realisation of cheating, breaking the law, washed over me. That I wouldn't want to win Julie in anyway ignoble. But it wasn't that at all. Weedy little thoughts came into my mind: did I have a licence? How was I going to convince anybody that I'd landed a fish the size of a porpoise on tackle put under strain by a stickleback? I declined the offer and for a moment Murphy looked at me thunderously. 'How can I take it back? They'll know for sure how I came by it. There's nothing I can do with it so you've got to have it.' Though much smaller than Murphy, I've always been stubborn headed and I refused again. With a grunt, Murphy put his boot under the fish and kicked it back into the river. For a moment it lay on the surface and then, steadily gulped in air and sank back to its original position by the tree roots. I watched it for several minutes until it decided to glide into deeper water where it slowly became invisible. I looked around and Murphy had gone too and I wasn't to see him ever again.

I brooded on all these events in the back of my parents' car on the long journey home. Days had taken on a whole new significance for me. No longer the usual drudgery of getting school work done, of wearisome bus journeys, of explaining nonsensical Latin grammar to the flagging Socket. No. Every day had been filled with the glitter of magic, with new challenges, new experiences and new discoveries. Oh yes. I knew exactly what I wanted to do for the rest of my life.

Snuggled up in the comforting leather of my father's battleship Rover as we drove northwards home I didn't then know what I was letting myself in for. How could I ever comprehend the worries that since have beset me when I only dreamed the dreams without a hint of the fears? It's a fact of travel writing today that emotions are kept in check, barely, if ever, mentioned. Obviously, I'm reading tougher authors than I will ever be, but perhaps the uncertainties that beset me lurk also in their own minds. Understandable worries — air crashes, snake bites and sickness. Ignoble worries: grimy toilets, meat full of gristle, fat or blubber, squeezing out the ticks or pulling an obstinate leech from my shin. Absurd worries: I'll run out of toilet paper, lose my air ticket, or suddenly develop appendicitis a thousand light years from home. Over the years there's come to be a sort of realisation of what I am and what I'm not, what I'm prepared to put up with. Illness, animals and insects, heat and cold and food that would make a dog retch I can all take in my stride. What I can't take though is naked, human aggression. Perhaps because I've found

myself threatened in the past I'm reluctant to have a bullet put in my brain now.

The days before a major journey are always frenzied and it's part of my neurosis that I'm for ever packing and unpacking, checking and re-checking. Did I pack my knife, a whistle, some rope, and playing cards? Have I got enough dollars? Enough loo paper? Enough clean socks? And then it's the hateful night before departure. The demon alarm clock glowing there in the dark, its spiteful little hands beckoning me on towards an apprehensive departure. Why on earth do I ever set it anyway? When did I last sleep more than forty minutes uninterrupted on the night before a big flight? To be fair, I like to feel that these wobbles of the spirit are quelled to some degree when I'm actually in action. After all, I've remained calm when faced with a rearing tiger only five paces away, calm enough in fact to attempt a photograph. I reckon I've been comparatively stoic in rafting accidents, plane crashes, car smashes and the rest but I'm always humbled by those I've hired to help me. Indian, Asian or Inuit, I've always felt clumsy and cowardly in their shadow.

Attempting this book has been good for me because it's taken me back to the rows of battered journals, records of my journeys. Reading them, I've been stunned by how much I'd forgotten and often how wrong my memories of events have been. Names, dates and marginalities I can accept but really big things either totally forgotten or absolutely mis-remembered ... how, for example, could I ever have forgotten falling off a cruiser in the Black Sea and bobbing around for half an hour before being picked up by a fishing boat? Without those diaries, often such a chore at the time, I couldn't even have contemplated what I'm starting now. Bless them. Ripped spines, stains of blood, sweat, tears and vodka. Mosquitoes squashed between their pages. Forgotten names and addresses scrawled indecipherably in the back ... did I ever remember to send the photographs? All those memories, both miserable and magnificent. I believe that over the years I've written them down truly as I've experienced them but, perhaps they've here and there been distorted by circumstance. But what are truth and history anyway but perception and interpretation?

And so, for the love of fish, and with bated breath, here I go.

CHAPTER
I

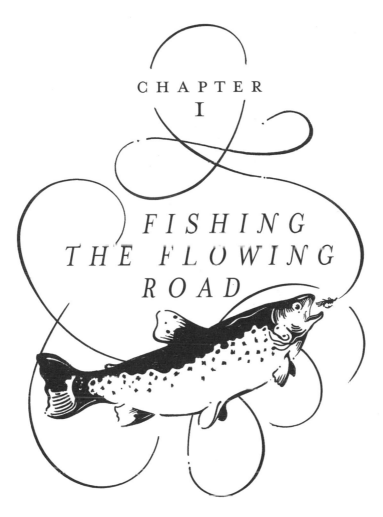

FISHING
THE FLOWING
ROAD

'Enjoy the adrenaline rush, these days so dense with experience that you live more vitally in a week than you do in a month at home. Every hour becomes a challenge, every minute a gift. But don't overdose on the action. Leave yourself moments for thought, for sifting all the experiences into their place.'

IF YOU'RE EVEN THINKING of embarking on the life of a traveller — an angling traveller or not makes not a jot of difference — there are plenty of things to get straight in your head. As a child, forty years ago, obviously I'd no idea of the fabric of an expedition, no concept of the logistics of travel and of how your sinews, both physical and mental, can be stretched nearly to snapping point. It's vital to know your limits.

'Hi John,

Yes, you're right. I have been to Murchison Falls, one of the few Danes, I think, to fish there. And I did catch a very large perch from the Nile. You must go. It will be the trip of your lifetime.

But, I have tips for you. Firstly, do not catch a bus at night. It's then that robbers lie in wait and many times passengers lose their possessions. You may camp close to the river but do take care. Do not go outside to pee at night because hippos will be around, big lawnmowers on the grass and they ain't no sugar babes!

When you do catch a fish, be very careful when you are landing it. Don't go near the bank, unless you have to because often the crocs will follow the hooked perch in and take a snap at it and, especially you when they get close to the bank. You can easily lose a leg. There are tsetse flies and these can be very bad at times. Their bites are painful but do not worry too much. Only one in twenty carries sleeping sickness I think.

Whilst I was there, there were sometimes renegade soldiers on the other bank and

24

occasionally they took pot shots at me as I was fishing. However, they missed and I think
they meant to. Perhaps they were only joking. I did have one bit of luck though. I left a
day early which was good for me because I later found out some thieves were plotting to
murder me and take my possessions on the last night. Phew, that was a close one.

Apart from all these things, there are no dangers and I know you will have a
marvellous time. Please tell me when you go and how you do.

Yours as ever,

Jens'

I didn't go. I've learned my limits. I know now that I can take
potential danger from animals, insects and sickness. I can withstand
extremes of heat and cold, hunger and thirst. For my age, I'm fit
enough and can walk a good twenty odd miles in a day with a heavy
pack but I don't want a bullet in the head thank you. Therefore, and
it shames me to say it, you probably won't find me in the Congo or
flirting with the womenfolk of the Shining Light.

If you do take to the travelling life, out of necessity you learn a
good number of things. These roughly divide into the practical –
simply keeping your being safe and the psychological, trying to keep
yourself sane. But let's start with the down-to earth and the basic
laws of survival. Obviously you do your preparation. It's fatuous to
talk about getting the right visas and injections but do check
carefully. I've only got two things of use to say here: firstly, it's not a
bad idea to take some spare passport photographs with you just in
case your visa should ever need extending. You're bound to need a
photograph and that's a little chore avoided. Secondly, don't get too
neurotic over the injection issue: if you believe some experts, your
body would end up looking like a colander for a simple trip to Goa.
Take good advice, keep calm and play the sane options. If you're
travelling alone, make sure you have some knowledge of the
language, some reliable contacts in the country you're planning to
visit and, above all, excellent maps and timetables. And, for
fishermen particularly, make sure your timing's right. Monsoons,

wet and dry seasons, early snowfalls, late springs and all the rest of these meteorological mysteries can really mess up a trip. Often fishing windows are small, grimy and can bang tight shut if your planning isn't meticulous.

When it comes to packing, I don't take many clothes with me these days. The ultra-modern, lightweight materials are a breeze to wash through every other day so you only need two pairs of kit along with some socks and a skeleton supply of underwear. Don't forget a tube of travel wash, though. It's one thing to look like a convict, another to smell worse. If you suspect it's going to be cold, simply stick in a set of thermals to wear underneath. Make sure you've got a completely waterproof shell as well and something warm and snug for your head, from where all the heat escapes.

Tackle is important because one thing is for sure: in most corners of the world that we'll be talking about there aren't any tackle shops. If there are, the best you'll be able to buy is a plasticine-type hook and a cork bob-float just big enough for a minnow. You'll need a spare rod, spare reel, a mile of line and an armoury of hooks. This is where your baggage weight will be critical so choose every item carefully for strength and durability. Buy the absolute best that you can afford and that goes for clothing and luggage as well as what you'll be fishing with. Five thousand miles out, you don't want anything, absolutely nothing, to let you down. Believe me, I've seen rods break, reels seize, hooks bend and suitcases coming back to London Heathrow tied up with neckties. I've witnessed waders leak, boots crack and waterproofs flood. I've heard people shiver so hard in inadequate sleeping bags that you think their teeth are about to fall out. So don't skimp and don't let this happen to you.

Think about unexpected items when it comes to your packing list: loo paper is the number one essential. There are as many airports around the world that don't provide it as do and once you're out there in the jungle, the desert or wherever, you're unlikely to find a

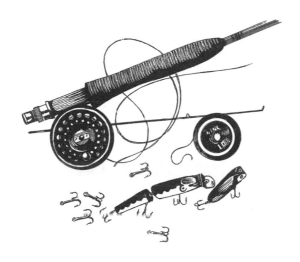

handy corner store. So, unless you want to do what the locals do and wipe your bum on a stone, grass or a passing lizard, take plenty of the white stuff. I know I'm going on about this but it's important … oh, and whilst I remember, an important tip. You're out there, miles from anywhere and you've selected a nice little spot for yourself with a good view over the valley and river perhaps. Down you settle and out in front of you lay your loo paper. But there's a good breeze and, at the vital moment, away waft the precious sheets. Keep them in a pocket. And for the sake of us all, bury or burn everything you've left behind.

Packing … some more essential items. You can never do without strong tape, whether to wrap rod tubes, luggage or coil round and round a Maglite torch so that you can hold it between your teeth. A small pair of sharp scissors is essential to cut things a knife just can't and because I can't whistle through my teeth, I always take a trusty Acme Thunderer in my pocket. You never know when you've got to attract attention. Talking about teeth, have a check-up before you go and pop into your bag somewhere a small vial of clove oil … this could save you or your companions many a sleepless night. Don't forget pens for children, especially in the Third World. Much better

than sweets though, sadly, the men throughout most of the globe will still be looking for a packet of duty-free cigarettes. If you make big journeys often enough, the chances are that there will be plenty of times when you don't have any common language with the people around. This is particularly gloomy at a night time campfire when you'll often find the locals decide to sing to you rather than talk. You have to reciprocate, which can be a problem if, like me, your knowledge of songs is restricted to the first line of half a dozen Christmas carols. The answer, quite obviously, is to take a song sheet. I can now quite confidently and proudly state that 'What shall we do with a drunken sailor?' is sung by the majority of guides on at lest four continents.

Check that your travel insurance is tip-top, up-to-date, covers the area that you're travelling to and extends beyond your expected return date. Take more money with you than you think you're going to need and hide it carefully in different places around your person. A good, strong, money belt strapped to the chest, under the shirt is a wise investment in many of the more dangerous countries in Africa, Asia and South America. Ensure you've got plenty of credit on your cards in case of emergencies abroad and whichever currency you're dealing in, take plenty of small bills. If you offer a twenty-dollar note for a bottle of mineral water to a Russian street trader, God knows what your change will come back in.

Get to the airport early. I'm personally neurotic about this and sometimes feel I'd like to camp out at check-in but if you can be first, the staff are fresh and, as yet, unhassled. Have everything that you need ready and always try to be 'nice'. Being helpful and appreciative can pay unexpected dividends. One terrible morning in Bombay, I was bargaining for six tickets on to Bangalore. It was 4.15, the flight was due at 5.00 and the supervisor was under siege from a couple of hundred of distraught Indians. And me. A particularly demanding gentleman, desperate for Madras, fanned his ticket so persistently under the harassed official's nose that my frayed temper finally snapped. 'Please, sir, give this gentleman a moment's peace. Can't you see he's trying to do the best for all of us?' An angelic smile crossed the supervisor's face. 'Give me your tickets now to stamp, sah. Hurry now to the gate and Godspeed your journey, my gentleman friend.'

I'm not saying for a moment that women don't do big trips but it's a fact I generally find myself living with men which can be pleasant or downright hell. When you meet a new team at the airport for the first time, look out for the snorers because you sure don't want to room with them. A snorer is generally overweight, frequently sporting two days beard and will be the first to suggest a swig of hard spirits early in the morning. Just for the stomach, you know. Medicine, eh? You can bet your last dollar he had his wife or fishing partner in the deepest of despair for most of the previous night. Watch how men behave when it comes to moving the team's luggage. Do they weigh in and help with everything or do they just shift their own personal items? How are they at queues? Are they relaxed about taking their turn or are they continually straining to be first? Do they ever pass round biscuits, a mint or two or are they content to take what others have to offer? Okay, we all eye up a pretty woman but who's the one that makes the lewd remark? Yes, the early signs of trust and friendship are easily spotted.

Mosquitoes. Midges. Black flies. Tsetse flies. Sand flies. Flies, flies and more flies. There'll come a time, perhaps soon, when you'll wish you'd never heard the word. I don't care where I'm travelling to, it doesn't matter how firmly I'm assured insects won't be a problem, I always put a bottle of Deet (or a similar substitute) and a head net into my luggage. Always. If you're at all suspicious, pack mosquito coils as well and a full length net if you've got the space. Remember to tuck your trousers into your socks at night and never, ever go for a poo around thick bushes, or in a hollow, or anywhere there isn't a breeze.

For me, sand flies are the worst...

DIARY ENTRY 18TH MARCH 1999 —
ACKLIN'S ISLAND, SOUTHERN BAHAMAS

'A night of pure hell. Sand flies biting all night. They got through the net. Like Scottish midges but not afraid of indoor life. In bed at 8.15 pm. awake and thrashing until 5.30 am. Plans for tonight.

1. Keep clothes on.

2. Get into a cotton bag and under the bedclothes.

3. Keep the room fan on.

4. Put mosquito coils in every corner of the room.

5. Spray the room with Deet.

6. Smear Deet all around the house.

7. Get into a bath of tepid water and breathe through a straw.

8. Cover entire body in layers of super glue.

9. Sleep in back of pick-up and get driver to circle the island all night.

10. Hire a Mr. Blobby suit. Or perhaps a pantomime horse outfit.'

The chances are that you'll be fishing with a guide who will either make or break your entire trip. If he's surly, lazy and useless then try to get rid of him. If he's young, eager and useless stay with it and try to encourage him. Hopefully, you'll find somebody dedicated and knowledgeable and treat him like gold dust. And with such words, we come to the delicate subject of tipping. Tip too much and you make a rod for your back and those to follow. Soon, you'll have a guide who won't get out of bed for five dollars and wants ten dollars to put the engine on the boat. Make it clear you'll tip at the end of the trip and that the amount depends on satisfaction. If there's a camp manager, ask him for advice. Go over the top and everybody suffers: Len was so pleased with his guide down in India he tipped him enough one night to leave camp, go off to his village and build a new house. When it comes to tipping, don't forget the ancillary staff of any camp — the cooks, cleaners and so on. They're all part of the overall picture even if not the stars. Wherever you can, why not give presents instead of money? I've already mentioned pens but, in colder climbs, fleeces, socks, gloves and the like are all gratefully received. Shirts and trousers are eagerly accepted anywhere around the Third World, none too clean or freshly laundered. For sterling service, how about parting with a cheap pair of binoculars, Polaroids or even an old Walkman that could become the village treasure? I once hiked a singing plastic fish — Billy the Bass bless him — seven thousand miles and he's still the icon of the village children. Stupid but fun and there's not much of that in some of their lives.

Should you give to beggars? Should you inevitably haggle over prices? Don't ask me, I just don't know. For what it's worth, I personally tend towards the compassionate here. I know that giving can encourage begging and dreadful things are done to children especially to engender pity but there are times you just know that the money is needed. It's just the same with haggling. I know, again, it is an accepted part of life in many areas of the world and I know you incur bewilderment or worse if you don't join in. But it's not always necessary. Or so I think. For the sake of a dollar or two you can make a big difference, in countryside areas especially. It's hot, you're tired, your stomach is queasy and your nerves are frayed and it's easy to be dismissive of the beggar or street trader but remember that this is their existence, their life, before you say no.

Big trips with a fishing rod beside you are, or should be, the best times of your life and you'd think you'd remember every single day with cut glass clarity, but you don't. The mind works in all manner of mysterious ways and it isn't long before what we perceive as reality is well and truly fogged. History at its best is an uneasy science and I really do find that it helps to take a journal. You don't need to write reams but the skeleton details of each and every day can prove vital for accurate reminiscences in years to come. Also, if you're ever planning a return, it's good to have the names of guides and friends at hand, that otherwise would have been long since forgotten. And if you are going back, take some copies of the photographs you took. It doesn't matter where you're going, you'll be welcome for that alone. I personally probably spend too long behind the camera: I work on an assumption of three transparency films a day which is piffling by National Geographic standards but can run up a fair development bill after a month's journey. Personally, I'm not into camcorders because you can't film and still photograph at the same time and I know which record I personally want to make. I've never seen an amateur made film that hasn't made a TV washing powder commercial seem riveting.

Take care of yourself physically. I'm not talking about being neurotic here but just watch your every footfall. Remember your accident can ruin things for others as well as yourself. It's a simple matter of responsibility. Drink one to two litres of water every day...this can be difficult on a non-stop bus, I know, but do your best. Try wherever you can to buy mineral water: go for fizzy because that way you know if the top has been tampered with. When you're in camp always make sure that water is boiled and add some flavoured vitamin-enriched powders to make the taste more acceptable. Throughout at least three-quarters of the globe, avoid ice like the plague. Drinking from streams? You can in Greenland but you can't in India so show sensible caution. Cleaning teeth? Hmm, I go for bottled but then I'm a wimp. But an alive wimp at that. I can tell you to be careful with alcohol till I'm blue in the face, I know, and it will have little or no effect. And as I rarely practice what I preach anyway, I'll move on to food. Ice-cream in everywhere but the West I treat as a no-no. So too fruit I can't peel. Give me nice, plain, well-cooked rice, dahl or potatoes. Where it's allowed and practical, cook the catch. Don't relax when you get back to a city and a deceptively grand hotel. The odds are the kitchens are twice as grubby as back at the camp and I'll tell you, whenever I've been sick it's been in a city bedroom.

Make it a habit to turn over your boots everyday and don't go near scorpions, snakes or other nasties until you're quite sure they're dead. Vic Sampson once saw a notorious ferdelanc battered to death by his guides and sported it the rest of the day as a belt. Back at camp, he flung the lifeless body over his tent and played cards with his companions. Into the second hand, they saw the coils unfurl in the lamplight and the head, which had been swinging day long by Vic's genitals open up and hiss venomously before sliding away into the darkness.

Let's say you do get sick, that gripe in the guts at 2.00 am, that greenness around the face by three and the desire for death an hour before dawn. Obviously try your own medicines first but don't be afraid of a local doctor with local remedies. There are times when you just have to put your trust in the hands of others no matter what your suspicions might be. Don't let yourself dehydrate: force down water or tea and above all, keep calm and try to find as comfortable a place to sleep as possible. Don't give up, don't panic and believe me, recovery can come as quickly as the sickness in the first place.

All that was the easy part. Nothing earth-shattering. Nothing controversial just advice hard won through forty major trips around

the world. The games that our minds play, however, are more elusive, obviously subjective and I should balk at the prospect of even attempting to prescribe good mental health. If you're healthy in body but sick in mind your trip will be ruined as surely as salmon run from the sea. And so, with all humility, here I tiptoe.

Patience, my friend. Patience at airports, at hotel check-ins, in camps, with guides who come from different cultures with looser schedules and unknown timetables. In the West, we're uptight with time, we've allowed it to become our master. Traffic jams, train delays, time wasters, so much to do, so little time in which to do it. Remember that an expedition is not only leading you to new waters but to new ways of life. There's a bliss in losing control, of being out of control, of realising you cannot influence the events around you. Say goodbye happily to 'normal' life — schedules, timetables, man-made things which we like to think we control. That can be the beauty of the big trip: away from our rigorously ordered little lives, we can come to realise that we control nothing at all, nothing of real importance. Do we choose when we are born, when we die? Rains, droughts, winds and snow? No. Pitch up in the Amazon jungle or on the Siberian plains and we're just human beings along with the other vulnerable, weak creatures of the earth.

There may be times, perhaps frequently, that you'll frighten yourself. My own private drama is with heights and I still recall, with a chill, a rock face in Greenland and an ancient bamboo suspension bridge across a gorge in Arunachal Pradesh that I always felt sure would turn turtle until I saw one man playing a guitar as he crossed it and another carrying a cow. A jaunt on a seemingly docile horse can turn into a nightmare, especially on the homebound leg when the creature gets a whiff of camp food. You hang on tight then let me tell you. Sometimes you might wade rivers beyond your limitations or be asked to raft through white water that makes your stomach churn. Or perhaps you'll have to scramble screes with rivers foaming

beneath, knees knocking. You question yourself: is it brave to go on? Or just foolish? I don't know and I've never made my mind up on this point but I do know that you can cope. I'm personally more afraid than the average coward but I've managed so far. Of course, I'm not talking about foolhardy things that no human should or could do but rather challenges quite normal to the people who are used to the environment. They might seem outrageously risky to a pampered 'first worlder' like you and me but sit back and see how

even the children cope and every horror settles into its own feasible context. And don't be afraid to ask for help: Batsokh, my Mongolian brother, invariably leads me over the single larch trunk bridges, laughing, yes, but tender beneath. On horseback, accept the offer to be led by an experienced guide if you're the least bit unsure of yourself or your steed. If you're asked to wade to that far rock then take the firm hand of your guide. Don't worry about looking foolish — it's better that than dead or injured, believe me. Remember, that if you've stretched yourself once, any physical demand will come easier the second time. Don't worry about the return journey over a bridge or a cliff face or whatever but push it out of your mind, forget it. Know that you've done it once and so you can a second time.

Everything gets easier. If you've pushed your courage to the limit you can do it again and again and each time you'll find the limit of your own personal bravery that bit more easily. Brick by brick you'll build up the wall of your personal stoicism and confidence in your agility. Don't over-reach yourself but don't do yourself down either.

Don't moan. If you're tired, hungry and cold the chances are everyone with you feels exactly the same. Keep any dark thought down and a calm front up. To moan will only increase any depression in those around you and reinforce your own misery. So, if you sense that the mood is darkening, why not try to lift it instead? A song might sound corny — bloody irritating even — but it can work wonders in a forest of dripping rain when every muscle aches for relief. So too does the popping of a beer can. 'A Beethoven symphony to my ears,' says Leo. Don't whine then but go for it. Enjoy the adrenaline rush, these days so dense with experience that you live more vitally in a week than you do in a month at home. Every hour becomes a challenge, every minute a gift. But don't overdose on the action. Leave yourself moments for thought, for sifting all the experiences into their place.

If you're homesick, don't be. You'll get home alright and within a day, by the time the bills are opened, the chores are sorted and work has begun, some of the most vital days of your life will seem light years away and you will wonder why you ever longed for the humdrum routine. Love, true, deep, young love is of course a different matter. Perhaps during these months — or if you are lucky, years — when you cannot breathe without the lungs of your beloved, you are best to stay at home. Or travel together, but then you're panicking all the while, solicitous to the point of neurosis over your partners welfare. Is she — or he, for this book assumes women are every bit as intrepid as men — too hot, too cold, too anything? 'Too' becomes a big word of your adventure which isn't at all how it should be. You might even begin to wonder whether love is going to survive. Is your partner seeing you anew? Are disagreeable character traits emerging under stress? Are habits that were endearing at home now becoming irritating under pressure? Or is she beginning to fancy the rugged, outdoor guide, or is he transferring his affections to the gentle, brown-eyed cook?

And, whatever, please don't be macho, not around me anyway. The big strides, the big tummy, the big voice, the big laugh, the big promises don't fool any of us. Let your actions do the talking for you and remember, nobody but a fool thinks that catching the biggest fish of the day makes him or her better in any way. If you set yourself up to be king or queen of the river each day, you're going to spend more miserable nights than happy ones. Trust me: I've been there. Rejoice in the glory and excitement of the captures of others and they'll celebrate sincerely when you land your dream. I mean it: when others are deeply excited for you, you can genuinely be excited for yourself.

Big trips like these should give you new values. Different things become important to you. Alright, the very best equipment is necessary for its quality and dependability but less and less for its label or its image. The clothes you wear keep you dry and either

37

warm or cool depending on the climate: it no longer matters whether they impress. You learn to do with the bare minimum: excess you can shed to those a thousand times poorer than yourself. It's easier for the feet and the spirit both to travel light. Giving away all your unnecessary chattels becomes as satisfying to you as a snake shedding its skin. You really do begin to value health rather than wealth in a real, not just platitudinous, way. Your health becomes everything, your be all and end all. 'Seeing' rather than 'possessing' begins to take precedence and in fact, you realise that most of the worthwhile things in the world you cannot possess anyway. You share that sunset, you can never own it. The river only lends its fish to you, expecting a quick and a safe return. These philosophies don't necessarily come quickly or easily and it helps if you travel with like-minded friends. That way sanity and selflessness build up more quickly, walking onwards hand in hand.

A personal neurosis: never say that anything will be plain sailing. Too many times I've thought that privately, deep down only to awake with a rude shock when the tail end of a journey carries a real sting to it. The air tickets that weren't confirmed, the plane that doesn't arrive, the stomach bug born on the last night... now, I don't celebrate or flush myself with success until I see my luggage come off the final carousel.

It can be strange coming home, like a diver coming up from the depths needing a decompression chamber. Your sleep patterns are disrupted so don't worry if your eyes open like saucers at 4.00 am each morning for a week because your body will readjust. Take care with food though and give your stomach a chance. Don't pig-out on your favourite, rich meals for a while if all you've been used to is plain rice for weeks.

The mind, though, is less easily cosseted. Sometimes, after a big trip, you return home and cannot begin to focus on the reality of normal life. Bills, phone calls to return, e-mails perhaps. Normal life, what is normal? This farce of periphera, or the world of sights and senses, challenges and emotions you've just passed through. You're home, wherever that is, physically unscathed we hope but for cuts, bites, aches and pains: spiritually though, you're in tatters. You'll enjoy a very short honeymoon period, your own bed, and the comfort of your possessions, a night out with friends, a real pint of beer in a pub where everyone knows your name. And then comes the void. The knowledge that each and every day won't henceforth be packed so densely with adventure and experience that you half expect your head to explode. There, so many things that happen in a day that you can barely unravel them all: here a week with its petty cares and concerns passes like a day. I remember how life was as a schoolmaster: term running into term as painlessly as sand pouring through an hourglass. And for me, just about as satisfying.

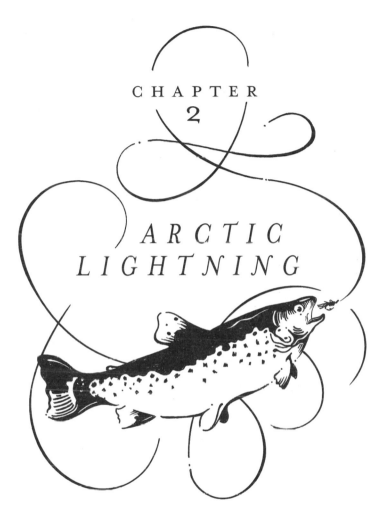

CHAPTER
2

ARCTIC LIGHTNING

'Paradise Valley is a place more undeniably close to god than most. The Inuits have always known it. The Americans sensed it. You'd have to be a clod to ignore it. Especially so at around nine each evening when the sun sinks to a certain level in the sky and paints the cliff face in a unique and heavenly light.'

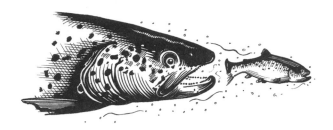

TOWARDS THE END OF JUNE, when the sun sets behind the fjords of Knoydart in northwest Scotland, it can catch the facing slope of Gairich and when it does so, it turns the mountain into a massif of fire. This occurrence doesn't happen every night by any means — there obviously have to be atmospheric conditions I know nothing about — but my observation suggests there will be no cloud, next to no breeze and the air temperatures will be falling rapidly. The surface of Loch Quoich — pronounced Coo-ich, as though a dove were calling its name — will invariably be calm with slight streaks of riffle at most — and the blazing mountain will be reflected gloriously by its mirroring waters. It is at precisely these moments — just on the wavering of the light — that the loch's population of char rises from the inky depths to feed on the plate glass of the surface. They ascend in their millions, dimpling the surface as though light rain were falling from the star-emerging sky. Perhaps they sip at the dead and dying midges, victims of the cooling air. Perhaps not, but the fact remains that these char are everywhere, these butterflies of fish, once sea going but trapped in the newly formed lochs over ten thousand years ago as the ice sheets receded. Butterflies of fish? Well, yes, char are extraordinary, some with tummies tinted lemon, others a rose blush and some males flash a red to challenge Gairich's sunset strip.

Char are delicately spotted, all with unique patterns yet perhaps most glamorous of all are the underfins, delicately traced in a glowing, creamy white. Char are exquisitely secretive. In fact, these are the only moments of the year that you'd ever realise the species existed in Quoich. The rest of their lives, they remain deep, often a hundred feet or more down, feeding on minute organisms that drift in the undertows that build up there during the protracted periods of gales. The char can be located on sonar, pressed together into packs millions strong. Probably there is safety in numbers, some protection from the mighty ferox, the great, predatorial brown trout that live only in these glacial lakes where char, their prey, are to be found.

It was ferox that had drawn me to the north as a lad, as soon as I could drive in fact and coax an ancient Fiat along roads thousands of feet too steep for it. Those were the first days when maps sent a shiver down my spine, when I delighted to spend winter evenings sitting round the atlas looking at splashes and ribbons of blue and urging my imagination to take me there. If you really are a traveller then a map is the most dangerous of things, especially a highly detailed one that shows tiny roads leading into nothing but wilderness, tapering away into a landscape that not even the cartographer knows a jot about. Not many people, ever, have known a great deal about ferox. Just a name. And the remoteness of the home address. And the mystery of a fish as rare as anything in the world. I was captivated (still am). Feroxide set in. The ferox had to be the perfect fish. There was almost exactly a twenty year time lag between the moment I first read about a ferox trout in the books of Victorian sportsmen and the moment that a hooked one finally slid towards my boat: plenty of time for my mind to fever with desire for the fish and to embellish it with all manner of miracles. I've always held that fish to some degree reflect their environment and this first ferox caught from the lunar-like west arm of Quoich, was as exotic and as otherworldly as any other fish I had previously gazed upon. On one level, to some eyes, the fish was just a trout. Of course its size, at ten pounds, made it different and special but there was more. So much more. Consider this. Ferox are a marvel of adaptation: over ten millennia they have learnt to forsake the diet of insects enjoyed by their normal brown trout cousins and original ancestors in favour of fish. Because the swarms of char exist, so can the ferox. If the char were to disappear, so would the ferox, there is not a more complete predator prey relationship in the whole world of natural history. The hunter certainly showed in the eyes and the hooked, toothed jaw of that first ferox, a brown trout endowed with the capacity to grow huge. It's extraordinary, as though a sparrow can evolve into a sparrowhawk or a mouse into something the size to threaten a cat.

It is because the ferox is a hunter of char that you will sometimes see them on glowing Gairich nights. On occasions the ferox will be tempted to forsake the gloom and come to the light for their hunting. The array of disco colours on the loch face will erupt as a pack of ferox arrow into a shoal of char forcing them to scatter like a carpet of needles. So quiet it is on nights like this that you can hear the swoosh through the hush, even when the massacre is happening half a mile or more away. You put down the oars. Drink it in. It's the essence of creation.

The drive down the track from Quoich back to the dear Tomdoun Hotel is a wondrous one now the light is veiled. Even at midnight in June you will be able to see deer dropping from the heights to feed on richer pastures. There will still be a glow around the mountaintops and most definitely a lamp on in the nearing bar. Gordon would never shut until the last of his anglers was in and their nightcaps requested. 'One for the ditch.' Always eager to hear. How big? What on? Whereabouts? All the usual angler's stuff but so sincerely meant.

We got married there, at the Tomdoun. Where else could possibly offer such mountains, such generosity and such an abundance of

44

ferox trout? When the rector embraced us he signalled the start of crazy days. The tiny kirk up from the hotel had not witnessed a wedding for over two centuries and ours was to be like an awakening for it. We were commanded to raid the manse garden down on the shores of Loch Ness for flowers to decorate the church. It was mid September — hopes of an earlier summer wedding had been dashed by a delay in Siberia — and the chrysanthemums had grown huge, blowsy, deliciously exotic and they filled the tiny church with deep, musky scents. We agreed a selection of jolly songs with the organist and on the eighteenth, some fifteen of us gathered before the rector who married us and then blessed us with a rousing rendition of the Skye Boat song on his mouth organ. This inevitably was the prelude to eighteen hours back in the bar where drink was drunk as only the highlanders can. Day turned to night and night to day again as wine flowed and stories were told. Peter sang. Johnny and I danced. Maddie the spaniel howled. Arm wrestling led to a fight. Folk came and went and returned again. Sometime after sun up the next day, a stalker broke his ankle stumbling on the coal scuttle and his family drove him away down the glen. Sobered, the party very slowly began to disperse. Some left on foot, some by jeep and a couple on horseback.

Shortly after this, I travelled even further north with Maddie the spaniel and his companion Christopher to stay a while in a bothy at the remote end of Fionn loch. The weather had broken up badly and for days on end vicious gales threatened to shake the little tin and wooden building to smithereens. We were crazy to go out on the water at all in waves that frequently threatened to overwhelm the tiny boat. They were particularly miserable times for Maddie for though I've never found a dog who loved and understood fishing nearly as much, he still hated the waves and the wet. Worst of all for him was the spindrift and whenever the boat were caught in a column of spray so dense we were lost to each other and he would set up the most mournful of howls. Sodden, bedraggled…if a dog can look off colour under his fur, then that was Maddie, skulking in the boat well, shivering under the coat designed and made up for him by one of his frequent girlfriends. Nor were things better for him back in the bothy: the foul weather had forced the stalkers in off the hill and each evening we'd find Jimmy, Dougie and Stewart in before us, stoking the kitchen range, steaming in their wet clothes, drams well under way. 'Soft wee doggy, in a cuddly wee coat,' guffawed Dougie each evening, lobbing a boot in his general direction, laughing as the poor dog slipped morosely down under the bed. Discretion Maddie quickly learnt to be the best part of valour and he'd only sniffle and snuffle a little when the sausages and bacon began to cook. A wet nose. A tit-bit scoffed and a brief, brief thump of his tail.

DIARY ENTRY 2ND OCTOBER

At last, I think the weather and Maddie both might have just turned the corner. This has been the third glorious day in succession and all his old enthusiasm for the job in hand has returned. He's had his nose glued to the rod tips for eight hours today. He actually alerted us to a take we hadn't noticed and then he barked grumpily when we missed it. Stupid, stupid human fishermen. We redeemed ourselves with a fine ferox of about eight pounds and we took his ecstatic yapping to mean we were back in his good books. He arranged the photographic session as he always does. Maddie centre stage, dog with fish. Eyeball to eyeball. Damp nose to cold snout.

The job in hand? Christopher and I were employed to catch and radio-tag ferox trout so that we could at least begin to build up the haziest of pictures of their movements. We didn't learn that much from Dennis (after Law), Jimmy (after Baxter) and all the rest but what did emerge was a sensation of movement. The tagged ferox would travel deep and they'd travel far. We might pick up Dennis by the island in the morning and then he'd be registering close to

the far end, five miles away, in the afternoon. So, are ferox eternal nomads, drifting on the sub-surface currents through the deep, dark water? Probably their only outlay of energy is to maintain their balance and their depth and they simply fin along with the current much like a hawk floats in the thermals. In all probability they only have to feed once a week, perhaps less and they can take their time, waiting until they sense a char shoal nearing. The fluttering of a million tiny fins reaches them through the gloomy water and begins to stoke the pangs of hunger. Then the ferox click back into life, begin to flex and to actively swim through the loch towards their prey.

It was during that good weather that the Northern Lights appeared over the bothy, rippling their shimmering way towards us from the west. We leaned against the old walls and watched. The stalkers even were quiet. There was nothing to be said. Our drunkenness focused and diminished in the cold. 'I only came out here to pee,' Jimmy informed us, 'and here they were. Everywhere.' Scotland could not get more beautiful. I'd seen it all, everything at least I was meant to

see. I'd witnessed awesome ferox, spellbinding char, scenes and people so unforgettable. And yet I knew there was more.

During the war, the Americans built a runway for their bombers along a fjord of Greenland's western seaboard. Sondre Stromfiord — Kangerlussaq in Inuit — is and was a barren place. The dreary streets that once housed an air force: the concrete-grey river that crashes its way from the glacier, under the bridge, muddying the estuary. Everlasting sunlight during the summer's height: eternal night in winter's depths. Today, the town is enlivened by periodic landings of international jets, generally from Copenhagen. The airport bar bustles, the shop opens. The restaurant does good business until two hours later the tourists have gone their own ways into the wilderness.

Back then, groups of wandering Americans found a valley different from all the others. The plain there was unbelievably rich in grasses and wild flowers. There were more animals and birds and the river held more prolific runs of bigger sea going Arctic char than anywhere else. There even seemed to be fewer flies! The Americans called it Paradise Valley.

Johnny and I arrived there in the summer following my wedding. Of course, what the Americans and we found was not an unexplored land but one that was sleeping, a place that the Inuits had known for five thousand years or perhaps more and had always recognised as special. There always has to be a most sacred place, even in a land as pure-as-chiselled-ice as Greenland. This is why the valley was the chosen burial place of so many ancient hunters whose bones and artefacts scatter the tundra to this day. Their shallow graves are everywhere, exposed by the endless winter winds and the armies of excavating Arctic foxes. Paradise Valley is a place undeniably closer to God than most. The Inuits have always known it. The Americans sensed it. You'd have to be a clod to ignore it. Especially so at around nine each evening when the sun sinks to a certain level in the sky and paints the cliff face in a unique and heavenly light. The day's wind seems to hush around now and in the gathering silence I truly swear you can hear voices. Saying something, what I don't know. Perhaps secrets from the past, loves long lost.

DIARY ENTRY 21ST JULY

Tonight we found the spawning site of the char. A rapid shallow run, perhaps fifty metres long with deeper pools beneath and to the side. Not an instantly dramatic piece of water to a man but obviously an hereditary goal to the char that make their way from the sea, along the fjord, up the river to this special place. I caught a large char, a male, magnificent in red and it had GOD written on its flanks. It did. Honestly it did. Tiny letters etched amidst its scales, visible as I held it in the current. I studied the fish in all lights, turning it this way and that before the sun. Sometimes faint, other times vivid but always G.O.D. Tooth of seal, claw of bear, scar of rock. Surely. Does the Lord sign any of his other works? And if he does, why not write in Inuit? Or Danish? Whatever, there's no denying this is a strange and wonderful place.

I'd hated Johnny for a while. I appreciated the need to travel light and the overwhelming necessity for warm clothing during nights that left the tents rimed with frost — sun in the sky or not. But to deny me more than one book, one bottle of whisky, one pack of biscuits, one slab of chocolate for fourteen days smacked of sadism. It was only after they'd all been consumed and that I'd been forced back into myself and my own resources that a light began to dawn. It was through those last few days that I began to feel a real closeness with the land, a proper understanding of the past. Once the biscuits and the whisky had gone, I found my satisfaction with char increased. Johnny and I didn't need anything else: the freezing crystal water from the river to drink and grilled char to eat — warm at night and cold for breakfast. We began to get on better and better too — always the deepest of friends but now developing a relationship where words were often totally unnecessary. We seemed to know instinctively when we'd want to sleep, when we'd want to fish and when we'd want to move on, exploring more of the river. Of course, not even Paradise is perfect. It was a constant effort to keep the pilfering foxes out of our tent, off our food and away from our rucksacks. Repeatedly, a gang would run off with our dinner as it was cooking and we'd have to go back to the river and start catching a couple of fish all over again. But, on reflection, perhaps that was not too great a chore! I was also chased by a musk ox, a bad tempered, evil-smelling old male (probably exactly what he thought of me) who thundered after me a hundred yards or so until I reached the safety of a major rock fall where the crevices halted his pursuit. Mind you, he continued to hang around the camp looking moody, occasionally pawing the dust. One morning we woke up and he was hoovering the grass around our tent. He eyeballed me furiously for a second or two before mooching off up the river.

It was up the river that we found Five Mile Pool. There might be a more special pool for char in the world than Five Mile but I doubt it. It's a run of perhaps a hundred yards, very narrow, very deep and absolutely crystal. It's close to the glacier and the char can get no further so it's a prime spot, one selected and fought over for æons by the biggest of the fish. The males lie there like eighteenth century soldiers, resplendent in their red coats. They're huge and they're angry and they're waiting for females so they can spawn and battle their way back to the sea. We caught only a couple of fish from Five Mile and they were definitely the biggest, most spectacular char I have ever seen. Of course, we couldn't eat fish like that, even if our own lives had depended on it — and to catch them for fun somehow seemed questionable. There was just too much going on around the

place, in our own heads. After all, Paradise Valley is so perfect because the Inuits don't net the estuary and don't hunt the animals. The musk ox, the deer, the Arctic foxes know next to no fear. They're wary but unafraid and we began to query our right to be in such a special place. We haven't gone back since, though we'd both love to and I know I dream about it all with startling clarity and depressing frequency.

Of course, there are other rivers in Greenland that are magnificent but they're somehow different. Don't laugh but though I've fished another dozen or more I've always found even the flies invariably worse! Just why I haven't an inkling but I tell you it's true. The flies can just get everywhere until they drive you mad, in your clothing, in your hair, up your nostrils. They wear you down and make for tensions in camp...

DIARY ENTRY 13TH AUGUST AMITSUARSUC VALLEY

The zips are really doing all our heads in. Zips, zips and more zips. This should be called zipping and not camping. But if you don't zip the flies just drive you mad. Jim goes for a pee in the night...you hear his sleeping bag zip, the inner tent zips, both of them, being unzipped and then rezipped. The same for the outer flaps. Then there's his trouser fly zip, opening, closing and then the outer zips doing the same thing. Inner tent zips, sleeping bag zip and all thought of sleep has been banished by this trail of angry hornet-like sounds chasing you from your dreams. And then, inevitably, Stew wants a wee and then it's morning and everybody's zips are up and downing like a crazy concerto written by a mad wasp. Can't someone invent a noiseless zip? Or a zip that has melody? Perhaps one that can sing a song.

Nor have I ever found fishing nearly the equal of that in Paradise. The reason is easy to see: on virtually all other river mouths, Inuits set up nets for periods during the summer and very early autumn, as the fish are running. It's their hereditary right. Families have been doing this for generations, for centuries and they know how many fish they can take and how many char they have to allow through to maintain the stocks. Unlike many hunters around the world, the Inuits aren't so blind that they destroy their own runs of fish. The char are essential to them: they smoke them and keep them as valuable nutrition for the winter months. The smell at the river mouths is often appalling. The guts of scores of char hang around in the short grass, barely visible through the clouds of clamouring flies. The smell of the smoke houses manages to be both acrid and sweet and mingles with the strong scent of salt in the air. If the weather is grey and drizzling, as it often can be, then the smoking takes forever and the smells become more acute. Clothes smell. Hair smells. The whole world, it seems, becomes stale and unclean. Many of the Inuit families can be resentful of sport fishermen, suspicious that our rod catches will threaten the run of fish up the river. It's important to stress catch and release and that only a few fish might be kept for food. Of course, there will still be a lot of char in their river but probably not as large as those in Paradise. Remember, it takes several seasons for a char to reach its maximum potential and every time it runs the gauntlet of those nets, it uses up one of its lives!

Animals, too, are more scarce because the Inuits are great hunters. I watched a man and his daughter pursue a deer over six miles or so of mountainous scree and marsh. The creature got to the fjord and leapt off the cliff, swimming towards an island. Both Inuits jumped into their boat, careered after it and shot the creature at point blank range in the water. They lashed ropes around it and pulled it back to the shore where they sat on the beach and butchered it.

There's still a great deal that probably nobody knows about

Greenland, certainly not me. There are hidden rivers and the secrets of a thousand lake systems. Adam, the boldest of all my Inuit friends, and I sat in the tent around midnight. It was dark enough to need a torch on the map because of the clouds cloaking the sky and the wind that was raging to blow the tent over the ice mass. We loaded more and more rocks onto the guy ropes and as sleep was impossible, we just sat and talked. Adam's finger traced a crazily winding lake system. 'Great big red fish, John. Perhaps they're land-locked. Perhaps they sometimes get to the sea. I don't know I've only been here once and I hardly know the place. But I tell you the fish are one metre long and deep and broad like fish I've never seen. To reach the place you need to kayak around the coast and then you camp and you live rough. Yes, much rougher than this. A tent. Fishing tackle. Nothing else is possible. We just live off the fish.'

I lay in the tent as it billowed and shook. This was the night that a camp to the north was half destroyed and a Danish friend, Peter, lost his boat in the fjord. I thought back to the storms I'd witnessed in my quest for char and ferox and all the wonders I'd seen. The Milky Way. Icebergs. Hunting whales. Even once, in the north, a distant white bear. Dinosaur bones and a Reverend serenading us on a mouth organ. I was living in a world when anything seemed possible.

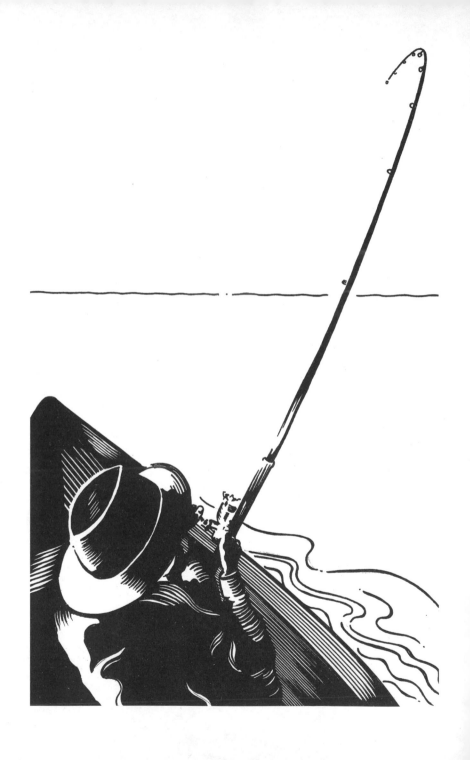

CHAPTER
3

SONG OF
THE STURGEON

'Sometimes, on the long row back to the boat, I'd see a
sturgeon hunting. A beluga, the mother of all the sturgeons.
Possibly the most awesome fish on the planet, creatures from the
crack of creation. They surged into the shallow water as they
hunted, their backs black against silvery, shivering water.'

MOCHANOV, WHO WAS A BEAST OF A MAN, was shot in the head, his body found in the winter Volga, just south of Astrakhan. He was big in the Mafia there and during the weeks that I spent with him, his stories chilled my soul. Many times I felt sure that he was just boasting, trying to cower me, establish a bullying sense of superiority. It was only when Pasha, my sensitive and humane interpreter told me one night that every drop of blood Mochanov mentioned had in fact flowed that I saw this toad of a man for what he was. Fat. Swarthy. Covered in a sheen of sweat and immensely strong. Evidently cunning to have led such a pack of thieves for so long and quite without scruple. Pasha told me what I'd already guessed at: he'd have squashed me like a fly had he not felt I could potentially be of use to him. With the deaths of scores/hundreds/thousands I can't guess, to his name, the demise of a single, squidgy Englishman would have made little difference to his sleep at night.

Mochanov and I were on his launch, cruising the Volga from Astrakhan down southwards to the delta looking at fishing possibilities for European visitors. In one sense, I spent three weeks in wonderland: a fabulously wild environment of untouched marshland, home to all manner of wildfowl, waterbirds, amphibians and of course fish. Carp, catfish, perch, zander, pike, tench, rudd,

asp — the list is endless and doesn't cover the tens of species I could not even guess at. And, what is more, nearly all grew to monumental sizes and were present in unbelievable numbers. It was the colours that struck me most, the fabulous pinks of the dawns and the burning red sunsets; Everywhere, too, lay the tapestry of old Russia or at least the shreds of it: girls picking tomatoes in the fields. Fishermen's communities amidst the islands clad with poplars, willow and alders. Nets drying and worked upon by their women. The men themselves were laying them, rowing them out from old wooden boats. Girls washed clothes over the side of houseboats and punts were ever on the move up and down the river, weighed down with thatching reed and farm utensils. Cowherds rode past now and again ushering their cattle from one swampy pasture to the next.

A fisherman's paradise all right ... 5 a.m., poling down an arm of the Volga. Vladimir, groggy as a bear, vodka still on his breath, anchors up on an arm of water three or four hundred yards wide. The water beneath is deep, green and greasy, an immense current of water. We're on a huge eddy where catfish are striking their prey in slow easy rolls. We catch glimpses of their evilly fat, mottled heads and then their immense tails coil after them. Feeding fish throw up trails of bubbles everywhere, sparkling necklaces on the seductive water. The sun is up. The sky is blue, horizon to horizon, broken only by lines of poplars regular as telegraph posts and it becomes hot almost instantly. The catfish action is incessant. Two of forty pounds. A near sixty pounder and a fish that looks a hundred pounds plus that breaks free just before breakfast after a killing fight in this thirty feet of powerhouse current. I feel as though my back, not just my line and nearly my rod are broken. Fun? I think not.

Some mornings, we'd take breakfast at a fisherman's settlement, in a lodge once said to be frequented by Brezhnev. He caught so many fish, they said, that he threatened to cut off all aid to the Astrakhan province. Let them just use fishing rods Brezhnev said.

Bottles of vodka on the table. Inevitably, too, slabs of cold sturgeon and bowls of scummy sturgeon soup. Warm, slightly rancid caviar and cabbage swimming in grease. Pasha comes close and tells me there is a rat running around the kitchen. I ask him why they don't catch it. 'How?' he asks. 'They bite.' I suggest a trap and Pasha looks blank. 'Another would only take its place. There are rats everywhere. Mostly in high office.'

In the afternoons when everyone on the cruiser slept, I would row off into the crystal lagoons off the main flow of the river, set deep within the islands. A small spinner would do, sparkling in the water and each cast would see perch, pike, asp, catfish, zander and even carp following in. Big perch. The biggest perch I've ever seen anywhere. Shoals of rudd swam past incessantly, golden as treasure. Bitterns fringed the coves, hunting for frogs and toads and ospreys slashed the water, taking large, struggling perch back to their nests.

Sometimes, on the long row back to the boat, I'd see a sturgeon hunting. A beluga, the mother of all the sturgeons. Possibly the most awesome fish on the planet, creatures from the crack of creation. They surged into the shallow water as they hunted, their backs black against silvery, shivering water. Here, a shoal of asp sheer away from a fish perhaps five or eight hundred pounds in weight. There, a carp of a full twenty pounds is seized a metre in mid-air. Its end is volcanic. Mochanov was in no doubt: 'The beluga sleep in the deep holes of the river during the day. Sleep, my friend, like all wise creatures. And then as the sun begins to sink they stir and they move and they hunt. Again, my friend, like all wise creatures.'

Evenings were always the same on the boat, everyone preparing for the approaching night. The heat below deck was overpowering after the burning sun of the day sickeningly intermingled with the smell of cabbage, soap and bodies. So, with the help of dear Vladimir and Pasha I'd prepare my mosquito netting on the decks.

This would have to be elaborate for, as Pasha said, 'By nine o'clock comes the first mosquito. By ten past nine, the first million.' No matter how much care we took, however, there'd be thirty thousand mosquitoes within the net by midnight and another thirty million trying to enter. My nights were spent immersed in mosquito lotion so thick that I felt like a jelly baby. It was hardly surprising that sleep was hard to come by and during the night hours, my eyes wide open, I watched more of Mochanov's operation than he would have cared me to know of. Throughout the daytime hours, his swarm of men slept vampire-like in the gangways, salons and cabins beneath deck but at night, these snoring, tattooed bodies were galvanised. Boats came and went like flying saucers backwards and forwards to their mother ship. Some were rowed, some powered by futtering engines. Mochanov spent most of the night on the forward deck, his radio transmitter crackling, always impatient, always hectoring and shouting. Sometimes my little Russian Napoleon walked past me just to check the little Englishman was hard asleep.

There existed a palpable sense of menace. All the boats had rifles on their decks, the men had revolvers pushed down their belts. Once or twice, there was a crackle of gunfire well away across the water and on one occasion the boats came back in a hurry and we up-anchored and steamed away into the darkness, all lights aboard turned down low. When I mentioned these affairs to Pasha he told me in hushed tones to mind my own business. 'I warn you not to take so much interest. This is Mochanov's real business, once the night has come. It's all about caviar. How else do you think he pays for this boat, for all these men? Why do you think we eat the stuff from buckets when to a normal man each mouthful is a month's salary? No, I warn you, you stick to your business and Mochanov will leave you alone.'

I tried with Vladimir the next morning, poled up on our catfish hole. I felt that over the weeks we'd built up some trust. For a long while, he said nothing but I gave him cigarettes, asked as ever about his wife and family and tried a second time. 'What I tell you, John my foolish English friend, you forget. Sometimes Mochanov's men catch their own sturgeon on lines of hooks set tight along the bottom of the river. But mostly they do not bother with this. It is hard work and dangerous and it is easier to pay gangs of poachers to do this work for them. So at night, the boats go out and pick up the caviar from places here and there on the islands, just little shanty places which are only home for a week or two at a time. Built just for the purpose. The sturgeon that they catch the poachers bring back there in the very early morning and through the day they prepare the caviar. Mochanov's men pick it up and bring it back here to be packed, sealed and sent off by fast boat to Astrakhan. After that, I just don't know. And I don't care. Don't ever say you know this. Don't tell or we're both food for the fishes, eh?'

One night, there was gunfire so loud and so close to Mochanov's cruiser that I couldn't be expected to sleep through it. Small boats were coming in quickly through the darkness and Mochanov was

60

giving orders for us to up-anchor. The engines were throbbing underneath the deck and when he saw me, he shouted and pointed for me to get down below. I joined Pasha in the saloon. He was very alarmed. 'It's the police. The sturgeon policemen. They've mounted some sort of raid. There was some fighting I think...' His voice trailed off as we felt the big boat swing into the current and head off full steam south. I was worried and I asked Pasha about my return to Astrakhan, the chances of me catching my flight. He shrugged. 'Mochanov is your concern now I think.'

Half an hour later, Mochanov himself swung into the cabin, glared at me and spat a few sentences to Pasha. 'He says that you must forget anything you have seen tonight. He hopes this little incident won't stop you both doing business together. He says it is just ruffians trying to cause trouble for him and that now we are going where they can cause us no harm. He asks you to drink vodka with him as evidence of your goodwill.'

Mochanov and I drank the rest of the short night away down there in the heat and noise of his boat. We had obviously outpaced any pursuit and his mood visibly relaxed and he grew more expansive. Once more he began to chide, boast and bully. He had caviar brought down to us: it was still warm and he guzzled it with his fingers, it greased his chin. 'It is important you and I do business, ' he said. 'Soon there will be no sturgeon left here on the Volga. Nor anywhere else and I must look for new businesses. No, no more sturgeon,' he mused. 'It will soon come the day when I have to eat little pink Englishmen like you.'

As I say, I'm glad they put a bullet in Mochanov's brain. The year before meeting him, I had got to know beluga sturgeon well and

61

fallen completely under their spell. Yes, I tell you, they mean the world, the absolute world to me.

Johnny, Niels and I landed at Kazakhstan in the dead of night. We were hours and hours late: Moscow interior airport had proved to be as shambolic as ever and an eleven a.m. flight had left sometime in the afternoon. It was a blunderbuss of a plane and needed to land on two occasions to correct mechanical faults ... and if an Aeroflot plane does that, you can be in no doubt the problem's serious. I'd obviously eaten something bad in Moscow, something that got to my guts with appalling rapidity and the moment we touched ground at Guryev I simply scampered for the toilets. An error, it immediately proved, but one I could do nothing to avoid. It was pitch black, the smell was absolutely overwhelming and when I turned on my torch I could see why. The building had no urinals, no toilets: men did whatever they had to do wherever they could find space clear enough to clamp the soles of their boots. Just as I eased into position a character, similarly debagged, hopped crab-like into the halo of light cast by my torch. The man was ferociously angry, shouting at me, clawing his way towards me, fist clenched, teeth grinding. Lord knows what I was supposed to have done to the man − I only knew what I had got to do. For half a minute we bobbed around each other, avoiding the pyramids of dung. I offered him some toilet paper and, seemingly appeased, he shuffled back into the darkness from where he'd come. Shaking, I told Johnny about the event. 'Don't be squeamish!' Thank you my friend.

An old bus was waiting for us, commandeered for the journey down to the Ural delta where it merged with the northern Caspian. We drove for an hour along rutted roads, occasionally seeing clusters of light break the blackness. The driver eventually stopped for a pee. The moon was out and we realised that we were on the head of an escarpment and beneath us stretched the seemingly endless delta itself. It was beautiful and strange and made even more so by the

volleys of sound coming at us, wave after wave across the marshland.
'Toads,' said Viktor, our guide. 'Spring is when they, they make the
love, you know.'

It was near dawn by the time the old bus stopped beside a bay — we
had been delayed by a police checkpoint along the route. Viktor
motioned us outside and there, on the water-skimmed mudflat
lurched our home for the coming weeks, the soon to be notorious
S.S. Beluga, lying drunkenly on its side. Everything was pretty drunk
on the inside as well: a party had been arranged to welcome us
though most of the revellers were passed out on benches, tables and
in every corner you cared to look. An ancient old man was brought
to meet me and shook hands vigorously, cackling. 'This man, he
likes the English,' translated Viktor. Oh my God, I thought, is no
land safe from our wandering tribe? 'English hunting parties, he
says, came here. Before the war. Before the Revolution. He used to
load guns for the English lords and ladies when they shot the duck.
He was only a little boy but he remembers everything.' The ancient
scrabbled around in a pocket and produced a coin for me. A mint-
fresh Victorian silver sixpence.

'You must toast this old man, it is very necessary, I think,' Viktor
instructed me, taking a grimy glass and pouring in at least four
inches of vodka. We held our glasses high and chinked them. The old
man spoke drunkenly for a few seconds. 'He says, God save the
English and the Tsar!' I'd drunk vodka before, obviously, but never
in S.S. Beluga quantities. 'No problem,' each and every member of
the crew said on the opening of yet another bottle. 'Necessary. It is
necessary,' each and every Kazakh would say over each of the scores
of toasts that punctuated life there. Perhaps vodka was necessary, to
dull that unholy trinity of odours — sweat, cabbage and urine. We
joked that the toilet hadn't been cleaned since Hitler's day and then
only briefly because they heard he was coming. Vodka made the food
edible and even the two stolid cooks appealing... they certainly were

to the crew judging by the noises reverberating from their cabin in the hours before dawn. In all my time in Russia and its provinces, I've never felt so close to the soul of this sad world. Every problem seen through the vodka glass seems to fade, at least until the monster is unleashed, and then, phut, everything is blown away. To those who say vodka has no taste, they're wrong: vodka tastes of freedom and even if only momentarily, well, those moments can be strung together if there's enough of the stuff. And to those who say vodka ruins lives, those lives have been destroyed already. So said Viktor, speaking with the sophistication of a Muscovite. And one who was drunk as a skunk.

The Beluga also triggered my obsession — albeit a very guilty one — with caviar. Though we were in a sanctuary for sturgeon and couldn't conceivably take caviar out (police controls on the track in and out of the delta were brutally strict) it seemed there was nothing to stop us eating it on the boat. The amounts of caviar that were loaded onto the table day after day were astonishing. There truly were buckets of the stuff. By modern western values I guess at least £20,000 worth or more was laid each and every day. Amounts to make your mouth water, your wallet wobble and the conservationist in you shudder. Our dishes were heaped at breakfast and at night. Sandwiches of caviar were made for the daytime, often as not left dry and rotting in the boat, fought over by the flies. With the hangovers we nursed every day, to eat anything to do with fish was ill advised.

DIARY ENTRY MAY 3RD

'Eat, my friends, eat it down,' Viktor is always saying.
'This is food of the gods. Nothing in life is better. Food of the rich. Food
for lovers. Food for the sick. Caviar is nothing but goodness. There is no
waste, absolutely none. Eat caviar alone and never do you need to shit.
No. Never.' With thoughts of both G. airport and the mosquito haunted
pail beneath us, believe me, we tucked into that caviar.

64

Catching beluga, I have to say, was not nearly as good as eating them. What does it feel like to catch a fish of three or four hundred pounds? Not much, really. It's gruelling admittedly and you're under a huge physical strain in burning hot sunshine. They don't do a very great deal – perhaps a few blundering runs through the shallow, muddy water and, if you really clamp  down, you can provoke a dramatic tail walk. The real drama is being amongst them, these vast fish from the dawn of time in such a bleak, primeval setting. It is impossible not to be aware that beluga are around your boat … volcanic eruptions of carp, asp, bream and zander – virtually every coarse fish you care to name, fleeing from the invaders. The beluga, the largest of all the sturgeon species, you see, come in from the Caspian in pods of twenty or thirty fish strong to capitalise on the spawning cyprinids. They come in like battle ships, showing their great scuted backs as they belly through water often only three or four feet deep. These are whales of fish, so unsuspecting, so susceptible to ambush. They lift the boat as they swim beneath and Pasha, our boatman, delighted in drifting his fingers overboard, waiting for a head to rear out and engulf them. Laughing, he would simply slip them from the toothless mouth.

Johnny and I boated six beluga sturgeon during our first day, fish between two and four hundred pounds. It was strange how the day began to turn sour. At first, it was all whoops of triumph and grins. As each fish was returned, Pasha would dip his finger in the water beside the boat and write liquid figures on the deck. 100, for example, meant a hundred kilos. At first, Johnny and I could hardly believe it … one biggest fish ever followed by another. And another. Endlessly. We nearly expired. We were sore and aching. We realised there was absolutely no skill to this whatsoever – all one had to do was dunk a lump of fish under the rod tip for it to be taken almost

65

instantly. We had had enough, we began missing takes on purpose. Pasha, too, was bored and began to sleep in the bottom of the boat. And above all, we felt pity for these great, trusting creatures. What right did we, petty pleasure seekers have to disturb the lives of such mighty beings, creatures that had been on the earth for so many more million years than us. As a result, we spent several days asking Pasha to pole us around the lagoons that we found everywhere off the main river courses. These were crystal aquariums, it was like floating on glass. Everywhere were carp, pike, perch, rudd, catfish, asp... it seemed as though my childhood fantasies to see every fish in the world could be satisfied in this one amazing place. Our chief joy was to fly fish for the rudd, vast, golden-plated things of three and even four pounds with fins as scarlet as the Russian flag that fluttered from the mast of the Beluga. Bitterns stood sentry around the bays — twelve on one alone. Ospreys dropped down from the skies to pick up an asp or a zander... from asp to zander sums up this heaving world of fish.

The vodka induced us to do some silly things — Niels hunted a beluga on a fly for example. He broke two rods, lost three lines but finally was successful by pursuing a fish to the sea itself and beaching it on the shore. This master stroke was what prompted our own big idea. It's an everlasting sadness to me that my first diary ran out only half way into the trip but Johnny remembers the next part of the story pretty much as I do — even though it seems far-fetched enough to be from the moon. His plan? My plan? I don't think either of us could tell you now but Sasha began by looking blank as we tried to explain it but then nodded slowly, finally enthusiastically. We shook hands. It was the night before the last day and we were Smirnoff-crazy all of us.

The next morning we goaded our totally wrecked boatman into taking us out into the main channel, not far from the sea in deference to the theory that the very largest of the sturgeon keep to

slightly deeper water. There we anchored up for around three hours, watching as groups of sturgeon howlitzered their way through the brown waters towards us. There were fish and birds of all sizes, shapes and colours everywhere. It was a marshland paradise, like being present at the dawning of the world, witnessing a huge, fundamental beauty.

Johnny pointed. This was the long-awaited monster that was at the core of our plans. She was a yard across the shoulders, very possibly more, a beast of a beluga and she was trucking up the river towards us, asp showering out before her. It was an asp, too, of perhaps four pounds that we had on our hook. We waited until the vast sturgeon was some five yards from the boat and then Johnny swung it out underarm for it to land with a smack on the water's surface a metre in front of the great fish's snout. There was one of those wonderful time-frozen periods in one's life and then the world clicked back into gear. The beluga tilted fractionally out of the river to take the asp in and the water showered off her back, her huge head looking pearly-silver in the soft light. Her mouth opened up and there was an audible smack as the asp was taken. Johnny waited some ten

seconds or so and then struck. Nothing happened. Nothing. We looked at each other and Johnny struck a second time but there was still this ominous, silent cold war. Then the whole river began to rock, eddy and swell and we realised that the mammoth fish was manoeuvring herself round, preparing to head back from the sea, dimly aware of her predicament. But this was in our plan and as she began to run, we ordered Pasha to open up the engine and to follow. We pursued her for half an hour until we reached the great sandbank that led into the Caspian Sea itself and twenty metres before us, the sturgeon levered herself across it and we saw her momentarily in all her terrifying enormity.

Out in the Caspian it was like being in a sweltering saucer, sweating in a steamy, murky sunshine. The vodka from the previous night hammered in our heads and our dehydrated bodies were crying out for mercy. The sturgeon, however, showed no signs of tiring. When we cut the engine, the great fish simply pulled us onwards at her own remorseless pace. Johnny and I took turns on the rod but we made no impressions on her, not over three hours, not after five. All sense of reality began to disappear: it began to seem as though we could swoosh onwards on this great sturgeon sleigh ride for ever. The lines that Longfellow had written about a sturgeon in his poem the Song of Hiawatha came to my mind and I quoted them out loud. It must have seemed manic in this end-of-the-world place.

From the white sand of the bottom
Up he rose with angry gesture,
Quivering in each nerve of fibre
Clashing all his plates of armour,
Opened his great jaws and swallowed
Both canoe and Hiawatha.

This is a fate that would have suited us: otherwise I felt that Johnny, Pasha, our sturgeon and I were to be bonded together for all time. There seemed to be no beginning to what we'd started and

I'm sure there would have been no end had not Pasha gunned the engine and powered us to the head of the monster, pulled out his knife and sliced the line at the hook. Both Johnny and I remember noting that the fish was four or five feet longer than the boat we were sitting in. Awe was displaced by a wave of disbelief and raw fury. There was a huge swell on the Caspian and a bow wave like the Severn Bore cutting a way off into the gold. 'Sun go down. Iran. Much danger.' Pasha pointed south, placed the blade of his knife to his throat and shrugged. There could be no arguing with him.

Here's the finale and Johnny and I have talked this over many times in Copenhagen and, again, we're both united on it. 'Well?' Johnny asked. Pasha sat quiet for thirty seconds, leaned over the side of the boat and wrote 850 in streaming figures on the planking. We'd been hooked up to a fish of nigh on two thousand pounds for more than five hours on what was little more than beefed-up carp gear.

A lot went on during those times on the Beluga but nothing competes with the majesty of that final sturgeon. There are few days that go by without my thinking of her since and that's how I like to see her, swimming strongly southwards still, her heart singing to be free. Yes, I'll say it again: I'm glad that Mochanov's dead. It would be good to think he serves as a warning to all those who would do these majestic creatures harm.

69

CHAPTER
4

MONGOLIAN ODYSSEY

'The best times to be in Mongolia? Night is special with the sky like a planetarium above. You're cold to your boots. Frost on the gers. The crackle of woodburners. Singing. Toasting, vodka glasses glinting in the lamplight. Wolves howling outside in the distance and the anguished barking of the camp dogs in retaliation.'

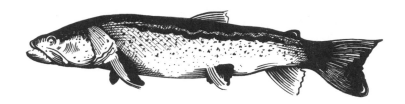

VIKTOR, SAID ONCE ON THE S.S. BELUGA that glasses of vodka are much like a diamond necklace in that one precious drop inevitably follows another. Certainly, there were very few nights on the boat when excesses of the precious liquid didn't make sensible talk impossible but on one of them, Niels Ortoft took me on one side. 'Let's talk,' he said simply and we left the fetid mess room and climbed the stairs to the deck. It was a wondrous night, so still, so silent, a crispness coming into it, a big moon beaming over the Caspian.

'You know I do business in Japan and also a little in China. Two years ago I was in Beijing dealing with four very wealthy Chinese businessmen who also fished. They put a proposal to me. Their idea was that we would fly to a grass airstrip, be picked up by jeeps and taken off to a river that they had heard about. They were very important people you understand and could make a journey like this happen. I agreed to the plan and just two days later we set off, landing in Russia, China or Mongolia I was never quite sure. You know how remote these places are...there are no real boundaries... no real way of telling. Anyway, to the point.'

The moon glinted off Niels' spectacles and illuminated the passion on his face. His hand rested lightly on my arm and he stared at me intently. 'It was a night much like this, John. The river we had

been fishing was broad, sluggish with big, deep pools and all we'd done was rise a few small trout and pike, nothing of any consequence. And then came this night of the big moon. Our cook told us this was the moment, he even used the words 'Killing time'. He rummaged amongst my tackle bag and came up with two monstrous dry flies — real haystack mayflies that I'd half tied for a joke once back in Copenhagen years before. He was determined that I should try these creations before the moon started to go down.

'It was very mild, not a breath of wind. The cook took me to where a big pool began to tail out into slightly quicker water. I stood on a rock casting the dry fly as far as I could and then pulling it back making a 'v' on the surface. Nothing happened for twenty minutes but in that glorious silken night it didn't bother me at all. Most of the time I was just gazing at the endless stars above. I could hear harnesses clinking and then on the other side of the river a camel train of merchants came into sight, travelling at night to avoid the heat of the day.

'I saw a bulge of water rise up behind the fly. Crazy. How do you say it, pandemonium? And there I was playing a mighty fish. It leapt, silhouetted against the moon, head like a dog shaking a rat. The merchants saw this too and reined in their camels to watch. The fish was so big and so fast I never thought I'd land it on the tackle I was using but I did after nearly an hour. There was cheering from both banks as I struggled ashore with my prize. What the fish was I didn't have a clue but by the lamplight we saw it was a taimen, a landlocked salmon, you know, a cousin to the huchen back in Europe. We weighed it on the camp scales. Sixty-two of your English pounds. It was enormous but there were two things that struck me. Firstly that crimson tail, glowing like fire, like fire. And then the head. Vast, with huge jaws and glaring eyes. It was a fish from the dawn of history.'

Hucho taimen. Blood brother to hucho-hucho, the huchen sometimes known as the Danubean salmon, today the rarest sport

fish in Europe. Like just a few other British, I'd try for hucho-hucho myself at times during the last two decades of the century but increasingly appreciated a host of difficulties in my way. For a foreigner to find huchen rivers in Austria, Germany, the Czech Republic or Poland is virtually impossible, so protected are this species. Every year big huchen are caught, but by locals with expert knowledge and unrestricted access to these very rare waters. Niels's story, however, brought back the surge of excitement I'd always felt for the species and the images of that fish kept me awake until just before dawn. I felt I would die if I didn't catch a taimen. In retrospect an interesting and almost prophetic sensation.

Back in England, it was easy enough to find books on the huchen, for scientists have worked with the species for decades. It is known that the huchen grows very large — certainly to seventy-pounds — but grows very slowly. It is a predator and, once large, the head of virtually any food chain. They can be reared artificially in hatcheries and attempts were made early in the last century to stock places as sublimely diverse as the River Thames in England and rivers in the Atlas Mountains, Morocco. The huchen is firmly in the salmonid family, the great adipose fin is testimony to that and it is extremely ancient. In fact, the huchen is the oldest living salmon. Apart from the taimen.

Research on the taimen, blood brother to the huchen, has been much more restricted and there are only a handful of books on the species often containing vague or inaccurate information. The geographical spread of the taimen is a large one sweeping through Siberia down through China and across Mongolia. There appear to be five closely related species, varying to some degree in size and sporting orange, red or even creamy-white tails. As to ultimate sizes, the authorities vary dramatically. Two hundred pounds is the wildest guess and perhaps a hundred pounds more realistic. The sea run variety in far east Siberia is probably smaller still.

74

Before the 1990s, few taimen had ever been caught by travelling sportsmen. Travel in China for years had been very difficult and there was a deep suspicion that most of the rivers anyway had been over-fished. Mongolia, too, had been closed and in the popular imagination was every bit as mysterious as Tibet. Everything seemed to point to Siberia as the most promising location, especially so as at this particular time Russia was opening its arms to the West.

Through the nineties I made five journeys to Siberia. They were all failures and as my desperation mounted, each succeeding journey pushed the limits. I began to feel that I'd waded so far there was no going back, that any and every risk was justifiable. And it was in that frame of mind that I travelled to Moscow on 12th August 1994. I met up with my German travelling partners in an expensive but shabby hotel on the outskirts of the city. Notable amongst them were Georg, a restaurateur, Olaf, a policeman, Christian, a successful industrialist and Michael, a man who more than most knew just how fickle Russia can be. We spent an hour or two talking taimen or rather talking lack of taimen. Not one of us had ever seen one even though we had a combined dozen trips to our credit. Perhaps this record of failure had left scars. Perhaps we'd come through so many disappointments we were prepared for the worst, already thinking negatively before we were even moving east. But, what I did know was that the moment Sergei, our fixer, entered the room that we were dead ducks, shot out of the water before we had begun. Sergei was thirty-ish, tall but with that potato-like Russian complexion that speaks of vodka, lack of vegetables and a profound misery. His sprinklings of acne, gold-capped teeth and stale breath didn't surprise me but I was not expecting him to be on a cocktail of drugs as well. Not on our first meeting. That was too much. 'You want girls?' he slurred. 'Why not? Boys then? Well, we just drink here perhaps or a nightclub?'

Michael was as abrupt as I've ever seen him and told Sergei in no uncertain terms that we were to be at the internal airport at six the next morning, ready to fly at eight. 'And, Sergei, you will be there! You understand?' Sergei was there in body, still wearing the same crumpled suit but whatever he'd been on the night before had slipped through his system and now he looked drained, barely capable of getting us through the never-ending formalities and onto the plane.

The nightmare of that journey east has never left me, so crucifyingly slow, taking in four flights over three days before we finally arrived at what we hoped would be our paradise. The first to Omsk, where we landed at midnight, was relatively normal apart from dinner of a dry cheese biscuit and a whole, unpeeled onion given to us in a sealed plastic bag. Surprisingly these were positively guzzled by the Russians: only lately have I been told that raw onion cleanses the blood supply of alcohol and prepares it for more, of course. The plane was unbearably hot and crowded but Sergei slept noisily throughout and awoke refreshed at Omsk, which was just as well. We were plunged into near chaos but Sergei, through a mixture of champagne, dollars and a certain oozing charm managed to secrete us away on another flight bound further east for Ulan-Ude. In the cold of the night, we carried our luggage across the airstrip and loaded it into the hold. We were joined by five young, pretty girls along with a single man in his mid-twenties, an Aeroflot cabin crew, making their way eastwards where they were to catch up with a major international flight. It was now 1.00 a.m., just an hour into one of the girls birthdays and party-time was called for. A table was made out of a couple of suitcases and six bottles of vodka and three of champagne appeared along with strips of sausage and cheese. Sergei clapped his hands and danced. 'This is to be good, great, my Western friends,' he chortled and as dawn haloed itself round our aircraft we were all as smashed as each other. By the time we landed at Ulan-Ude, one of the girls had declared undying love for the tall, dark Olaf and had to be physically peeled off him. We all heard how well Sergei had done for himself in the deep, dark recesses of the cabin and at his jaunty best, hunted out our next flight onto Chita.

Chita is a depressed and dangerous place and when we landed there in the late afternoon, dehydrated, exhausted, dirty, ravenous but otherwise in good spirits, we realised there was little chance of catching our next flight even further into the wildernesses of this vast and creaking empire. There was no way onwards and we knew we were doomed to a night in downtown Chita. The evening progressed in the way any practised Russian traveller might predict. Barely had we shut the splintered door of our hotel room behind us than there was a knock upon it. Outside waited two drooping prostitutes with their Mafia pimp and we paid them twenty dollars to leave. We found a badly lit, badly smelling restaurant down a back street where we ate typically uninspired if not exactly nauseating food and then narrowly avoided a punch-up with the local drunks who followed us out into the road. Later, the quiet of the night was punctuated constantly by barking dogs, rasping motorbikes and once a scream which was ended by a single, sharp revolver shot. We were happy to be at the airport a little after sunrise, our spirits matching Sergei's who had foxed in at five. 'The chicks here are so sexy...'

Our plane on to Chara was an old twin-propeller job and once again we carried our own luggage on board. I shared a bench seat with a woman in her fifties clutching a goldfish bowl in which swam four Shubunkin-like creatures, one of which was in severe trouble. We waggled our fingers in the tepid water to try and give it some oxygen but it wasn't until Georg tipped in half a bottle of lemonade that the creature seemed revitalised. The lady opposite me with children and gold teeth gave me an apple. A Lenin look-alike watched us with undisguised scorn and then, happily, the engines burst into life drowning the howling of dogs and babies and we were airborne for Chara at last.

Chara airstrip — unlike the squalid town itself — was a wonderfully airy place. Tiny and remote maybe, surrounded by mountains and perched on the edge of the desert there was a space there that we enjoyed for the six hours we had to wait for the arrival of our helicopter. The heat grew intense and the woman in the control tower who sold us two bottles of mineral water for a ten dollar note cackled hugely. Swarms of great black beetles drifted in on the winds from the desert and settled on our clothing and luggage. An increasingly drunken Sergei watched and wagged his finger. 'They bite like dogs.' Just as Georg was bitten and remarking that a wolf was nearer the mark, we heard the sound of an engine in the sky and looked to see an ancient, yellow helicopter approaching us, wafting through oil plumes. Now, we were really on our way.

I've spent a good deal describing the horrors of the journey to our river in southeast Siberia so you might think things couldn't get any worse. You would, of course, be wrong.

As the helicopter first wound its way along the river valley distancing us from Chara we were stunned by its remoteness until, out there in the wildest of wildernesses, we flew over a factory belching smoke with a small town around it. I think a chill entered all our hearts. This is what we had all seen over and over wherever we had variously travelled throughout the continent. Though the river beneath us showed a breath-taking variation of deeps and rapid, white-crested shallows, we had that near-certain knowledge that its stocks would have been exploited, even if not decimated. No matter how vast Siberia is — and it certainly is — you can be sure that nowhere is left virgin, that everywhere has been picked over and left depleted.

We saw a cluster of tents with figures waving alongside and our helicopter swung down towards a broad, sandy beach. With the rotors roaring above us, we piled out and scuttled through the turbulence with our luggage. The pilot waved, grinned and spread out the fingers on his left hand twice starfish-like. He'd be back in ten days. As the air settled, a noise even louder than the departing helicopter began to emerge, softly, distant at first but growing nearer, louder, more savage by the second. We all realised the horrible truth: we had landed in the mosquito capital of the world. They were to make virtually every second of the next ten days a misery for us. There was barely any escape from them whatsoever. We only had one mosquito net between us — Sergei had sworn we wouldn't need them — and at times we were driven to take refuge in our tents but the days were too stiflingly hot to exist long under canvas. What Deet and Jungle Formula we had with us was soon gone and we were forced to swim in the rivers or wrap wet towels round our heads. Nor did night time provide any let-up to our physical miseries: once the sun sank, temperatures plummeted with frost forming before even true darkness had set in. Our tents that had been furnaces during the day turned to fridges before the first stars began to twinkle. Night after night we were forced to spend awake, sitting round the campfire, stoking it high until dawn broke and then, within minutes of sunrise, the mosquitoes would be back.

By the nature of the beast, taimen and good food rarely go together but here supplies ran unnervingly low. We had brought Gennardi with us as a hunter but his nearest success was to wound a wild goat which he pursued before being driven off the kill by an enraged black bear. Our rice, bread, jam and butter we found to be infested with ants or soiled by rodents and cockroaches. Gennardi did find a secluded valley full of blueberry bushes but the luscious fruit had attracted in the bears who regarded it very much as their own private harvest. And if we did manage to snatch a few handfuls, the effect of the blueberries on an empty stomach was painfully obvious and immediate ... and who wanted to take his trousers down more than necessary in such mosquito-thick air?

Had there been fish in the river, our prayers would have been answered but there weren't. The fishing was terrible, as bad as

anything I'd ever experienced before in Siberia and that was saying a great deal. Tyre tracks networked the tundra leading back towards the town and we found nets everywhere, old and discarded or new and recently used. Once again, we were foiled. Once again, we had come to the ends of the earth and found it rifled. All that had survived were grayling of a hand's length or so. And we had to target those grayling or we would simply have starved. Georg, Olaf, all of us forced each other out day upon day to fish for these tiny creatures knowing our lives and the lives of the camp staff depended on them. Most nights we were rationed to three or four sardine-sized fish each and if the day had been particularly fruitful, we might get six. There were occasional bonuses, my three-pound lenok trout and the burbot that Gennardi netted from a backwater, for example. Burbot though have the texture of wood pulp and the taste of old socks.

A trail from the camp led through the forest and up onto a hilltop, which gave commanding views out over the river valley and towards the mountains that bordered Mongolia. We trekked up there whenever we could because the breezes kept at least the worst of the mosquitoes away. There was a grave there. In 1901 the son of an English merchant had fallen off his horse into the river, contracted pneumonia and died and been buried to spend his lonely eternity looking out over this lost landscape. He and his father had been dealing in furs, which they bought from the local Evenk hunters for alcohol. As Sergei told us and as Gennardi sadly agreed, the Evenks, then as now, will sell anything for vodka. 'It's impossible to find a pure Evenk girl,' Sergei would say gleefully. 'Give her a bottle of vodka and she lives with you a week!'

But we were a sturdy lot and morale remained high until about the eighth day which Christian had spent in his tent too miserable to move. To make matters worse, Georg had lost a good lenok just under his rod tip and there was a general feeling that we could all end up like that merchant's boy, lost in a hush so deep that you could hear your bones breathe. Gennardi came to the rescue. 'Three miles below this camp there is a cliff beyond which we have not been able to go. These rocks are a barrier to us and to hunters both and the pool beyond it is untouched, I believe. Perhaps it has been untouched for ever. If we take a raft, we might be able to sail beneath the cliff and then somehow, walk our way home.'

We looked at each other. Given Gennardi's track record we doubted his ability to row us across a village pond but then sanity hadn't been high on our list of priorities so far and we decided to try it. The next morning, our grizzled hunter appeared pulling a craft behind him that made any Heath Robinson device look like a model of order. We crept aboard and followed the river down. In truth, the journey wasn't nearly as terrifying as we'd led ourselves to believe. Within forty minutes we were beaching at a magnificent pool some three hundred yards long and about eighty across. The depth looked unfathomable and the water had a mysterious green-grey look to it as it curled and muscled over rocks and beds of weeds. We fished with frantic determination, sensing we were close to something special and though we didn't actually catch any taimen we saw one.

Just after mid-day a great, streamlined, malevolent-looking creature swirled in from the depths after Olaf's spinner, patrolled the shallows at our feet for a full forty-five seconds and then

disappeared. We realised both that taimen are magnificent and that they are not just the stuff of legend.

We did find a way back to the camp that night and the helicopter did arrive to take us back to Chara, albeit twelve hours late. And it was in Chara that I had another seminal experience. We had supper at Gennardi's creaking, collapsing house and afterwards I asked to use his dunny. He led me down the path to the hut and there, above the thunder-box, a taimen tail was nailed to the planking. Its span was just over ten and a half inches and when I asked Gennardi about it he took me to one side. 'That was a huge fish I netted just over five, maybe six years ago. A hundred miles to the south, just through the mountains into Mongolia. That's where there are still taimen. Giant taimen. There are sharks there. That's where you really must go.'

In the years since I sat there on Gennardi's dunny, contemplating that tail and the soft autumn light outside, I have been fortunate enough to find that taimen paradise. It lies further than a hundred

miles from Gennardi's garden fence however — more like four or even five hundred — and it's situated more west than south but the important point is that it does exist. My own heaven, the place I thought I would never find, is set amongst mountains, snow-capped from mid-summer onwards, a range I've become overwhelmingly sentimental and protective over. I see those mountains as sentinels, guarding this fabulously pristine world from the rubble that Siberia has become. From our river camp you walk half a day or so to a ridge that's approximately two thousand feet above the flood plain. It's a difficult and demanding journey but the result is spectacular: from this elevated point you can stare straight down the throat of the mountains and along the gorge that the Shiskid River has forced through them in its eternal journey northwestwards. The flood plain itself is broad in places, narrow and rock-strewn in others, but almost always heavily forested and completely without paths — certainly to the north. This is a hundred mile corridor to Siberia untouched by man, unchanged for millennia. Not quite true: this is an irregular hunting ground of the Tsaatan, the legendary reindeer people, or at least the remains of that tribe which now has sunk to as few as forty members. In-breeding and uncertain sanity almost certainly will spell their end before long and one of the hardiest of all hunting tribes will be no more. Almost definitely, though, no Europeans have ever travelled the whole route of the Shiskid. Certainly, over eight years, my companions and I have done no more than nibble at the edge. The river and its mountains remain a world of secrets, mystery and beautiful other-worldliness.

Everything certainly looked that way on the evening of 27th August when we, the Mongolian team of two thousand, gathered in the mountain's lee to give Frank Pearson's ashes to the river. Frank had been a vibrant member of the '98 expedition and his death had been a huge blow, not only to the travelling Europeans, but to the Mongolians who had responded to his zest for life and captivating

sense of fun. Now eight of us were walking over the hill from the camp that he had loved so dearly to the large inlet in the eastern bank of the river. For two years we had known it as Frank's Bay: with us we carried his ashes in a small, gaily-patterned box. This was the last leg of a journey from Norfolk, through London, Moscow and on to Ulan Bataar, to end in this remote and beautiful resting place eight hundred kilometres to the northwest of the capital. This was the place that Frank had specified in his last letter in which he had also tried to explain his actions. But no matter how we attempted to kid ourselves, deep down we couldn't either fully understand him or help but feel he should have been with us in the flesh, in his enormous entirety. Over the weeks he had spent here in '98, Frank had been a whirlwind of activity: fishing, riding, arm-wrestling long into the night, teaching the children English, English songs and, essentially, cricket. Every experience he wolfed down, mulled over and packed away for what life was left to him.

At the water's edge, Rob spoke beautifully about the team spirit of '98, how Frank had been central to that, a conduit for all the energy and affection that flowed so freely between us and the Mongolians that year. How he had been there for everybody in everything: the first to offer items of tackle, to buy the first of the evening beers, to speak the first congratulations or, if necessary, voice commiserations. For those who had known him, Frank was there with us: those who hadn't met him believed they felt him close. Men like these, willing to go so far, are cut from the same cloth. I then spoke of the moment Frank saw his first really large taimen, a fish I was playing. We were wading, him burbling about the mountains, an eagle overhead and me, steely quiet, concentrating on a big fish pushing me to the limits. As it neared, Frank didn't see it, wasn't really watching anyway and then the fish rose out of the river in a roar of water, flaring its scarlet gills the way big taimen do. 'Bloody hell,' he croaked, staggering for the shore. 'Bloody, bloody hell, it's enormous...'

Jan said some words in Czech, wishing him peace and then Leo took the box and gently let the river lap away its contents. That would be the end of the story but the sunset over those sacred mountains took on the most volcanic reds any of us had ever seen. Not only that but the deep violet clouds to the east also began to glow, ringed in startling crimson, pulse after pulse across the night sky. Frank's farewell? Sentimental men, tears in our eyes. Mongolian magic.

Batsokh, our Mongolian brother, did not attend. He could not, he said. His heart would not allow him. Nor was this the Mongolian way: when someone dies here, the body is quietly buried in a scraping of earth. The headman then rides to the nearest settlement to report the death and to get drunk. The next headman travels on to the next grouping to carry the news. And so on and so on, riding, lamenting, drinking and returning until no-one anymore has heard of the deceased and the job is considered done. Batsokh in Mongolian means literally 'strong axe' and it is to him that I owe virtually everything I've ever experienced or achieved in this country. It was in Batsokh's ger — the white, round, traditional tents of the Mongolian's — that I first lived. It was his wife who initially fed me, his horses who carried me up and down the river. This is a man who has shown me taimen pools that can only be called historic, probably the best in the world. This is the man who has led me across bridges a larch-trunk wide, has eased my way over cliffs and even saved me from a closing pack of wolves. It's Batsokh who has taught me what little Mongolian I know, who has lit my woodburner in the freezing dawn and stoked it through endless

starlit nights. It's with him I've laughed, a couple of times cried, danced, got drunk and even had him anoint my bottom to soothe it of saddle sores. It's with Batsokh that I've enjoyed some of my greatest adventures.

As a child, I adored tales of derring-do, especially if they could be linked in any way with fishing. That's probably why I remember so clearly one of the most evocative of all journeys in angling history — the one so wonderfully described in the fifth edition of The Compleat Angler in 1676 when Isaak Walton's original manuscript was added to by Charles Cotton. Cotton contributed a section on fly fishing much of it in the form of a true adventure. Viator was described riding from Essex to do business in Lancashire. He's overtaken by Piscator, Charles Cotton himself, near Ashbourne in Derbyshire. The two men fall into conversation and Cotton leads the way twelve miles over the hill to Dove Dale and his own mansion. Now here's the rub...Viator is terrified...darkness is closing in...the 'mountains' seemed vast...the landscape deserted...his shirt sticking to his back...he fears for his very life as he descends the slope towards the River Dove. Then Beresford Hall emerges and

Cotton's servants appear to bring supper and sack. The ordeal is suddenly over and Viator can sleep between crisp sheets smelling of lavender and dreaming of sport to come.

So what? What on earth has this got to do with Mongolia? Or with me come to that? I suppose ever since I read this tale — not making much of the seventeenth century language to be quite honest — I'd taken parts of it with me. I'd always thought of recreating something dramatic and sinister for myself, a relatively safe little play in which I could enact the part of Viator. A fishing adventure perhaps that would leave me perspiring, gasping and in the same state of terrified awe as Viator back in late seventeenth century England. Well, Mongolia offers an endless panorama of possibilities for this sort of thing and, with Batsokh, I feel as though I've done everything Viator did. And perhaps more.

The times I've spent with Batsokh have been rich in experience and, with his keen eye and hunting abilities, he's pointed out a huge amount of wildlife to me. Wolves aplenty, wild camels, boar, elk, deer of all sorts, eagles, huge owls, yes, with Batsokh I've seen them all during our expeditions across the plains. Once we entered a forest straggling along the river and from the trees were hanging dead lenok trout, tied by their tails with pieces of colourful rope. I found it alarming as though I'd stumbled into some sort of pagan festival but Batsokh laughed at my fears. He explained that we were moving through a bear trap, that hunters would net a shoal of lenok and drape them out like this to entice the bears in. The longer the lenok swung in the wind, the more their smell permeated from the river and up into the rocky crags where the creatures lived. After a few days, the hunters would take up their positions, lying in ambush for days or even weeks until one of the giant animals came close enough for the kill. And, of course, we'd seen bear evidence aplenty ... huge prints, tree trunks torn ragged by claws, areas of grass the size of tennis courts flattened where a couple of bears had rolled their fleas away. But the true, living bear…never. Batsokh left me under no illusions: if I really, really wanted to see a bear then it would be to the north we would have to go, following the cliffs to that heavily forested piece of valley that only the Tsaatan knew much about and Batsokh, he admitted, just a little.

We left a little after dawn — a horse each for me and Batsokh and one carrying fishing tackle, guns and various baggages full of clothing and food lest we find ourselves marooned far from home. It was a glorious morning, the sun rising quickly and powerfully through a blue sky, the last of the frost melting under hoof and the mountains tipped in brilliant white snow. Soon we left the wide open plain, cut through the woods and then drew up onto a steep path destined to lead us through a canyon of towering cliffs and crags. Like Viator over three hundred years ago my shirt began to stick on my back as I stared uncomfortably down the ravine, a thousand feet or more to the forest floor and the riverbed. However, it was full daylight, the horses were sure-footed and Batsokh full of song. So, as ever, I trusted myself to him fully.

Around midday, we began to drop from high altitude into the most deserted of forests cut through by tributaries of the main river. We pulled the horses up at a small pool and I caught a lenok trout that Batsokh filleted and cooked, delicious with handfuls of herbs growing around. After eating, Batsokh pointed a way to the north, through the larches, to a vast rock fall with boulders like houses. 'Bear,' he said simply and shrugged. We mounted up and rode on into the gathering gloom of the thick forest. We had seen no sign of man now for well over four hours and we were simply following tracks through the dense trees created by elk and deer. Progress was slow and I felt the day beginning to decline, the heat going out of the sun.

It was around two o'clock in the afternoon when we got close to the rock fall. The forest was thinning out, giving way to species of Scots pine and silver birch whilst the floor was spongy with thick mosses and fungi. It was like walking through a gingerbread wood looking out for Hansel and Gretel. The smell though was heavy with the odour of animal, as though a hundred dog foxes had been along the trail. The horses too were becoming so nervous that we had to dismount and lead them onwards. Soon we found ourselves crowded around by rocks and trees — one of them had been slashed apart and stood ripped quite open. Unmistakable claw marks ran its entire length. Boulders had been turned over where creatures of huge strength had rooted for grubs, lizards and roots. There was hardly any sound, we were too deep in the forest for the winter reaches and could hear only the slightest trickling of water down the rock faces around and then I heard it: a low rumble as though a thunderstorm was brewing a hundred miles away. Batsokh was tense. The horses whinnied and pulled away. We stayed stock-still and through the gloom, perhaps forty yards off, two bears were watching us from over rocks and fallen trees. For minutes the seven of us — bears, men and horses — stood frozen and then, gently, Batsokh waved me back, gradually retreating the way we'd come.

We broke out onto open ground, got onto the horses and galloped away laughing and cheering. The tension had been broken, the deed had been done. Like boys out of school, we celebrated. Batsokh raced me to the main river to a pool he had visited years before — and what a pool it was. The river ploughed through a gorge, foamed white over huge boulders and emptied out into a vast body of eddying water perhaps a quarter of a mile long. It was one of these places that you know instinctively, without any shadow of a doubt, that you will catch a fish. And so I did, fourth or perhaps fifth cast. The taimen took, like all the big ones do: for a second you think you've hit bottom and then the rod tip begins to nod. A volcanic explosion of water. A flaring of huge blood-red gills. A body and mind-draining fight: and finally, there the fish was, an enormous orange-tailed creature lying on the sand before us. Taimen, the

most ancient of the salmonid family, every bit as wild, as primeval as the forest around. Batsokh held the fish and momentarily light gleamed along its flanks, then, as it slipped back into the water, clouds enveloped the sun.

Batsokh stood up looking at the sky, watching the clouds. 'We must go. We must be fast.' Rarely do you see Batsokh without a smile from ear to ear and it was with a chill in my heart that I remounted. The wind began to rise in the forest and by the time we'd cut up to the mountain path, the light was draining from the sky. The sun had disappeared and white clouds were rolling in from the north, from the vastness of Siberia. I glanced at my watch – nearly six in the evening and only two hours of daylight remained. Batsokh pressed grimly onwards.

We had climbed perhaps a thousand feet when the first snow hit us, dense, white, sticking to our clothes. Now it was impossible to see the valley floor beneath or the mountaintop above and the tiny pencil-thin track before us seemed to melt into the general whiteness. The pace of the horses slowed from a trot, to a walk, to a shuffle. Stones squirted from beneath their hooves, rolled

themselves in snow and dropped away into silent infinity. Huddling himself against the storm, Batsokh simply forged on before me.

Oh, Viator, if only I'd known! If only I'd sympathised and not laughed at your fears! Why haven't I been content with my life and its simply pleasures? Now this was a life I was in dread of losing. Who would find my body, who would mark my grave? Why had I played with my life in such a dreadful place? And for what? A childhood dream?

I thought I heard a wolf howl and then Batsokh turned round, the first time for an hour, smiling broadly. What? He pointed upwards and I could see that the cloud had thinned, now only a veil and the moon was riding high. Batsokh was singing and talking again as we left the mountain and galloped freely once more over the plain back to the gers and the warmth of the woodburners.

Exhausted, I lay on my bed, sipping at soup and the vodka bottle alternately. 'You scared?' Batsokh asked. I nodded. 'No, really? You no scared with Batsokh!' but I had been both terrified in the lair of the bears and whilst giving myself up for dead in the snowstorm on the mountain path. Mongolia, I knew, was a hard place, a place for hard people and perhaps over the years I've misjudged my own capabilities. Haven't I seen Batsokh's children playing barefoot in the snow and the ice of the river margins? Haven't I met members of the Tsaatan tribe, men who sleep outside on winter nights as a matter of course — even when the temperatures tumble to minus fifty degrees Centigrade? Over and over, I've questioned who I am to measure up to these people, especially when I visit simply for adventure and sample what for them is a way of life.

The best times to be in Mongolia? Night is special with the sky like a planetarium above. You're cold to your boots. Frost on the gers. The crackle of woodburners. Singing. Toasting, vodka glasses glinting in the lamplight. Wolves howling outside in the distance and the anguished barking of the camp dogs in retaliation. The murmur of the river and the occasional sound of horsemen passing through

the night. But nothing can be as spectacular as dawn in Mongolia when the rising sun strikes the mountains to the north and draws the valley out into an explosion of mist. The children play outside the gers and the smoke from the chimneys rises in a drifting, vertical column. The horses are being collected and led over the frost-spangled grass to be tethered and saddled. The dog is asleep, frost in its coat. There's a smell of soup, of chopped wood and the first eagle is in the air. The wane of autumn is a spectacular time as the larches turn green and then gold, startling against achingly blue skies. Days when sunset comes quickly, when the great fireball drops over the mountains and temperatures plummet from plus twenty degrees to minus five degrees in minutes. A period when storms can pick up out of nowhere, when temperatures do crazy things and you lose the sky almost instantly in a drape of white. The mountaintops flicker and blur and then they're lost. The larches bend before a gale. The fleece comes out of the bag and within minutes the world is a white-out. The wind drops and you can hear the river through the muffled silence. A dim orb appears in the sky, lighting up the mountaintops, fresh draped. Within two hours, the plain is clear and the larches are softly dripping. Just a taste of what winter will bring, a season in Mongolia that is barely imaginable. A time when it's too cold to leave the ger for more than three hours at a stretch. A world of frozen white, short, brilliantly lit days and endless, biting, moonlit nights. Communities huddling down in the folds along the mountains' lower slopes, places protected from the full blast of the wind. Livestock corralled, wolves without. Six months of isolation and only the deeply frozen river offering any route to the world outside.

And then spring, the time that the valley is at its most magical. What I've heard is that the ice on the Shiskid melts around March or April time and by May there is a carpet of blue flowers laid across the plain. It's then that the taimen in their battalions forge from the main river many miles up its shallow, crystal-clear tributary, the

Tengis. Somewhere in the mountains there is a lake and from it gushes a stream, a foot or so deep, over large, polished stones. When the taimen horde reaches the mouth of the stream, they turn up it and climb as far as the lake itself. And here, in the very heaven of the world, the taimen spawn. Huge fish, their deep scarlet flanks and orange sweeping-brush tails thrashing the thin water to a foam. Perhaps because of the appearance of the taimen, the Tengis has become a spiritual place. Shamans and the Tsaatan tribe come to the valley and all manner of visitors draw in to meet them: nomads, townsfolk, the sick and the suffering who have heard of the river and what it symbolises. Gers are pitched, fires smoke and the aroma of cooking mutton, beef and yak drifts in the wind. Children play and shout, dogs bark, horses gallop here and there, throwing up clouds of dust as they're spurred up by their riders. Camel trains come into view as merchants hear of the gathering and make their detours. At night fires begin to crackle, wrestling matches break out and soon the sound of innumerable songs fills the starlit night. It's a scene from the Mongolia of Genghis Khan. The mirror of the thirteenth century paintings you can see in the art museums of Ulan Bataar. People in Mongolia are few and scattered and always have been so. They're used to solitary lives, alone in woods, deserts or mountains and they relish these moments when they meet family or friends. News is spread. Young men look for the wives of the future — courtship can take years outside Ulan Bataar. Eventually, the taimen begin to leave the river and make their way back to the Shiskid to feed hard on lenok and grayling. This is the signal and the Shaman follow the fish, disappearing back into the wilderness. The gers are packed and the Tengis plain and valley are all but deserted again.

Lest you think that I don't see the problems in Mongolia and that I'm blinded by its beauty, well, yes I do. Let's take the Dadahl, the town in northeast Mongolia famous as the reputed birthplace of the great Genghis. There you'll find a sad, deserted, drunken place with the great statue of Mongolia's most famous son now rarely visited. It's a place of freezing winters and baking summers. No cinema, no opera and no library. TV programmes on a few flickering sets appallingly banal. Dadahl is a grinding place to live in, a town of ever-disappearing employment. There's lack of investment and if an engine breaks down there's no-one with the knowledge or the parts to repair it. That's why lorries rot in the ruts, their rusting bodies picked over for any items of use. Mongolians know that it's a near-impossible dream, for a woman, especially, to get on in life. There was a café in Ulan Bataar called, well, let's call it the Art Café. Evenings would begin there sanely enough: around nine there would be chamber music or a girls' quartet or some songs from a Russian opera or musical. By eleven the Russian men had arrived, something about the suits gave away their nationality. It wasn't that they didn't fit exactly or were tacky or even old-fashioned. It was as though the men and the clothing didn't belong to each other, rather like their unnatural gold-capped teeth that shone in the lamplight when they smiled. And they most often smiled when the girls had arrived. I couldn't say if Mina was typical, whether she was telling us the truth or even if this were her proper name but this is how it happened one night. She'd spoken to three of us in halting English, blessed with the Mongolian lilt on so many of our words — the way a Mongolian girl says John, even, makes you think you are possessed with a name of the gods. But if Mina's voice were lovely, it is quite beyond me to describe her beauty. She possessed that tall, slim erectness shared by so many African and Asian women who know what it is to walk many miles under hot suns carrying heavy burdens. Strength with delicacy. Her hair was long and black-brown to her waist. High cheekbones. Eyes impossibly deep brown. Lips full, made moist by the tip of her pink tongue. She was twenty-two she told us. 'I have to come to bars like this. I study art at the university. But money? No, there is none. Not for living. Not for studying. Not for me any way but this way. I not like Russians but ...'

The three of us danced with her in turns throughout the night, feeling her tight lace dress against us, the silk skin of her arms. Not one of us tried a kiss even, perhaps just a nuzzle of her hair. At the end, we each gave her twenty dollars and she looked quickly away a tear in her eye. But it wasn't enough. She came back to our hotel later in the night with two Eastern Europeans, members of a mining expedition. We found her next morning in the foyer, looking older, a bruise developing under her right eye, on that hallowed cheekbone. I know there is not a paradise anywhere on earth, that we men bring good and harm in equal measure and I believe the three of us pray for Mina anywhere she might be, for anyone she might have become.

CHAPTER 5

TROUT AT TEN THOUSAND FEET

'Gold mahseer are arguably the kings — or should it be queens.
Scales like flowing gold that simply explode in the sunlight
but, by a nose, I lean towards silvers. The scale colourings are
slightly more subtle with a hint of pewter and even turquoise
in bright light. But the tails ... oh, those tails.'

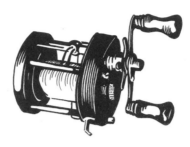

I HAVE EVERY RESPECT FOR YOUNG BLOODS ON FIRE, angered by injustices. Not every problem is soluble and peace is not everywhere negotiable. It is easy to believe so, reassuring to think we live in a tidy world but differences can be so fundamental and hates so strong that disputes can be inevitable and eternal. Even in centres of conflict, however, there are normal people, with different perspectives, who don't have the luxury to risk their lives because they're responsible for more than themselves. In every war-torn area there are those with spouses, children, dependants, businesses, lives that need to be run. And, whatever the rights or the wrongs, it is for these people that I feel.

Kashmir, back in 1989, on the eve of the troubles, was a precious, fragile place that you couldn't help but realise was in the gravest of dangers. Shooting around the city of Srinagar at night, bomb attacks, an exploded bridge, a bus queue sprayed with machine-gun fire left none of us in much doubt that anarchy was just around the corner. Today, I wonder what could be left of a country you could only marvel at. Mr. Gofhara will certainly be gone. Sadly, I guess, dead and gone. It seemed, all those years ago, that his old heart was broken and the thought of him surviving the wreckage since is quite impossible. Mr. Gofhara was a tackle dealer

with a faded but still elegant shop on the Srinagar Bund, that broad walkway alongside the oozing River Ghelum. When his father — or was it his grandfather — founded the establishment back in the very early twentieth century, the capital city was a very different sort of place. The Bund then was the focus of Anglo-Indian social life: army officers, civil servants, politicians, engineers, forestry officers, surveyors, road makers, educationalists — all those who made up the fabric of the Raj — would make their nightly strolls along the broad pavements. Warm summer vacations spent away from the heat of the baking plains. The best of times taken with family and friends, hiking, hunting and, of course, fishing.

Mr. Gofhara told how the colonels would come to buy their flies and spinners before heading to the Himalayan streams and he had the faded, sepia photographs to prove it all. In those days, the fishing in the high melt water rivers was quite wonderful. Trout, big, sturdy browns, of over ten pounds in weight were hardly to be wondered at. Catches of mahseer, perhaps not big fish but special all the same, were counted in their scores. The Gofharas in those days prospered. Agents for Hardy, Alcock's and Sharpe's, the tackle that they sold then would excite collectors now half to death. But, by 1989, Mr. Gofhara's shelves were all but bare. The colonels had long since stopped coming and the few visiting foreign anglers tended to bring their own gear anyway. Americans had picked over the best of the remains and made off with some treasures at criminally low prices. Whoever had told Mr. Gofhara this had only served to make him feel more cheated in life. Sad, lonely and afraid his empty shop echoed with the ghosts of sporting history.

In 1989, Dr. N.A. Jan, still, however, maintained his court. Dr. Jan was a very important man, not only was he head of the fisheries department, an honour in itself, but he had also written a book about fishing which showed to his superiors (not many of those) and his countless inferiors that he was a person to be taken seriously. His office was in a huge rabbit warren of a place staffed by countless clerks, secretaries, cleaners and guards who lounged around in every corner smoking cigarettes. We were made to wait for some while before seeing Dr. Jan but we had expected this: after all, as I've said, he was a very important man. At last, we were shown to his office, a warren of a room bursting with desks, scurrying people and every sign of frenetic bureaucracy. There were piles of paper everywhere, desks cascading in notes, permits and maps. A large fan whirred noisily above, occasionally lifting a slice of paper and blowing it to a corner of this frenetic bureaucratic world. Dr. Jan got up and shook our hands enthusiastically. He was a genial man in his early fifties, I guess, probably proud to be somewhat overweight — a mark of his prosperity — and he immediately presented us with copies of his book, duly signed. I still have his badge of honour in my bookshelf: a slim volume entitled Trout Angling – Kashmir. It contains a list of trout fishing beats under his control, some faded photographs of historic successes going back to before the First World War. A couple of pages on knots, the rules and an intriguing section called 'Tricks and Tips for Better Fishing'. The thirty seven points that follow show you how to avoid a 'jerked' knot, a 'kinked' trace and a 'bashed-up' rod and proved to us all that Dr. Jan knew his onions.

'So, my English friends, you want permits for the Rivers Bringhi and Lidder? Beautiful rivers. Believe me, you will think that you are fishing in Paradise. We have hatcheries full of very fine fish. Native bred. You will find everything still very much in order, I promise you. Ah, but money. That is a problem here. We do not have nearly as many people fishing as we once did and sometimes... sometimes...it is fine when people are kind enough to make some sort of contribution.'

Judging by the pumping handshakes, we paid handsomely for our tickets to fish Rivers Bringhi and Lidder but the money was well spent indeed and I guess I was among the last of the foreigners of the

twentieth century to cast a fly onto waters uniquely special. But, I wonder if Dr. Jan has gone the same way as Mr. Gofhara and whether he still has a department to manage or if he has eased into a sad retirement. The government of Kashmir now has more on its mind, I guess, than trout fishing.

Mr. Ramu's business must also be in trouble. He was a prosperous Indian gentleman owning a whole fleet of houseboats on the extraordinarily beautiful Lake Nagin, one of the sheets of water that made Srinagar such an elegant city. Mr. Ramu owned some monumental boats, Edwardian in design and exquisitely turned out with the finest carvings, most luxurious carpeting and chandeliers in the staterooms and each of the three enormous bedrooms. It was good to escape the bustle of the city, get back to the boat, settle on the verandah with a glass of cool Kingfisher and watch the sunset over the water. Traders poled their boats past constantly, offering silks, rugs and jewellery. As the light went, the bats took over from the birds and the carp around the boat began to sloop and slurp in the weeds ever more noisily. Dinner was served by Hari, the houseboy, a full seventy years of age, and it would be invariably delicious, all the ingredients bought fresh that morning from the various water markets. One night I remember so much gunfire around the city that it sounded like fireworks across the water, a light show in the sky. 'This is madness, sah,' Hari whispered serving out the rice. And, speaking for himself and Mr. Ramu, very probably he was right. What has happened to them now that the Europeans, the Americans and the Australians have been kept away for over a decade, withholding their bundles of dollars?

We got to know Sundar, our taxi driver well, tall, distinguished and the proud owner of two gleaming, spotlessly white Ambassadors. He based his trade around foreigners, they paid well, they tipped well and their faces were proof against the countless roadblocks around the city and its environs. Sundar liked talking with Europeans

especially — he had relatives somewhere near Birmingham — and loved to glean gossip on the royals and Mrs. Thatcher. He drove us impeccably for weeks, would wait outside restaurants until after midnight but then be there polishing his windscreen before any dawn that we might need him. It hurts me to think of him now, his cabs full of Kashmiris, squabbling about prices, sticking gum on the back of those forever dusted seats.

It was Sundar, of course, who drove us across the rice-carpeted plains towards the hills and the rivers. On the Lidder I met Narayan, my watcher there. He was employed at a few rupees a day to guard his own designated kilometre of water and to accompany me as ghilly on unforgettable days. No snagged fly was lost when you were out with Narayan, no matter how impossible it appeared to climb the tree or dive to the offending rock in the deepest pool. We met up with Dr. Thapa, in charge of several men and an extensive fish hatchery. But who goes there now with a fishing rod and who is there to hatch fish for? No ticket money, no tourist taxes and no hard currency. This is an economy with its foundations shaved away and I wonder, when I return, as I surely will, will I find the rivers miraculously preserved? Perhaps the trout will have grown on, huge, gullible and numerous, having benefited from one or perhaps two decades of neglect. Much more likely, I fear, I'll find the hatchery a crumbled memory, the river watchers scattered and gone along with their trout, poached by countless famished villagers.

And will it be the same on the Bringhi, even more lovely and remote? Will Rhaju's job be gone up there now? And Dinesh's? They loved that trout-rich river to the last polished pebble. Not that they were ever easy those trout, not in the burning heat of the day anyway when fish after fish would come to inspect the fly only to turn away with a flick of the tail. There were some big fish... I will never forget a team of six to eight pounder browns lying in a Bringhi pool. Everything began to change, however, when the sun sank, the air cooled and the women came in from the forest with their bundles of

wood. In those hallowed half hours, I do believe it was the best fishing I've ever known. Perhaps I've fished clearer waters for bigger fish but the feel of those dusks was so seductive, so aromatic and so utterly gorgeous it was easy to feel that you'd gone to heaven.

I belong to one of those few cherished generations in this crazy, violent world that has avoided war so I can't begin to fully understand its enormities. Nor do I take politics seriously: in Britain, all my adult life at least, one party has seemed much like another — taxes go up. Nor, being white, do I understand much about the horrors of racism. Being nominal Church of England hardly entitles me to diehard religious views either. But, even though I might be seen as apathetic, liberal, bourgeois and self-serving — I do know this: a ghilly in Ireland, a river watcher in Kashmir, a water bailiff in Yugoslavia cares more for the safety of his family, the prosperity of his village and the fatness of his trout than he does for a thousand pronouncements by politicians. The only sharp steel he likes to feel is the tip of a fishing hook. The only army officer he wants to meet is retired or off duty, with a rod and not a rifle in his hand.

There's a voice inside a fisherman that sings out at the sight of a shrine, a truly great pool: Paul Boote and I both knew when we saw the Black Rock emerge from the middle Ganges that we were there, at the core of India's mahseer-fishing past. Our journey from the high road down the steaming valley sides with our army of porters, horses and mules was an epic for me but nothing new to the ghosts overlooking the sacred spot where the Nyar tributary meets the mother river. What must the Black Rock have witnessed over those last decades of the Raj when mahseer loomed so large? Morris Metha, one of the ramrod backed military heroes of those fading

times, knew and did his best to tell Paul and me one monsoon-thrashed afternoon in his soaking home town of Dehra Dun. Once there had been many a troop like ours: officers and gentlemen had tramped whole wardrobes that torturous five-mile trek to the Rock. It's a life we cannot guess at now, an age that has slipped out of our understanding and, as men like the noble Metha die, the links are further severed.

There must have been great times at the Rock. We had them certainly and perhaps in part because of the film that Paul and I made there, great times are being had there again, I hear. Mahseer, you must understand, are not like any other fish. Everything about them is so intense that they bring out the heaven and the hell lurking in each day you live. I was so woefully naïve that day in September '89 when I hooked my first, around eighty yards or so beneath the Rock. Oh my, how these ghosts from the Raj laughed, how they rocked and rolled to see my complete and utter foolishness. They knew what I did not: you don't fight mahseer, they fight you and you're going to have to be tough to survive. But then, hadn't their life of struggle in this steaming subcontinent prepared them for the massive piscatorial challenge in ways my own had not? Metha and the others were men, toughened in a teak-hard environment. By comparison, my own hands and heart were lily soft.

My diary of those days well over a decade on makes unhappy reading…the humiliation those first three fish heaped on me…my

total inability to pick up a gauntlet thrown down by a 'mere' fish. So too my reaction to the maelstrom of emotion that haunted those extraordinary five days by the Rock when the fish finally decided to run. It had been a very trying time. The monsoon had lingered on that year ensuring that the Ganges ran high and coloured at a time when it should have been fining down. As fishermen, Paul and I knew that there was little we could do: the film makers around us understood and were sympathetic but still had a product to make and the pressure grew hand in hand with the soaring temperatures. Confidence in one's own abilities and the whole feasibility of the project was bound to wobble but I still feel I'm struggling for excuses. A lot of money and many reputations were riding on that film along with several putative careers. Half a dozen men and one very admirable lady were sweating in a melting pot environment and we had to succeed as a group and, I guess, individually. After a dozen days devoid of action, I lost three fish in an afternoon when, like a light switch being flicked on, the mahseer appeared suddenly and dramatically in the lee of the Rock. Stripped spools. Mashed plugs. Hooks not out of place in a museum of modern art. Truly, a floundering fisherman. There was another big fish lost two days on when my wits had returned and I thought I'd be able to cope. A fifth breaking free on the very last evening after I'd played it for forty minutes to the shore makes me realise I'm the worst of mahseer guides you could ever have! Funny, those five fish still swim through my dreams but I suppose it was meant to be. The Black Rock was a place of testing for us all.

I'm quite aware that to talk about losing a clutch of fish in this way can sound pretentious. After all, I'm not talking about war here or famine or galloping pestilence. Even if the mahseer were to prove my own apocalypse, it was I who had sought them out, and been destroyed for my pains. The Black Rock is for men tough as teak. For years my private late-at-night-hero had been Jim

Corbett: if you don't know about him you should, for Corbett wrote the scariest, spookiest nature books ever. *The Man-eaters of Kumaon*, *The Man Eater of Rudraprayag* and *The Temple Tiger* all display the extraordinary bravery of a man prepared to hunt man-eating big cats. A courage of the Metha sort, a kind of objective look at danger where you look at death in the eye through a long lens that in a strange way de-personalises it. Or if Corbett did feel fear — and who in his right mind would not have done — never ever would he have shown it. Not when he realised that the leopard that had killed three hundred people was stalking him and not, as he had supposed, vice versa. Not when he felt the eyes of a killer on his back as he walked down the moon dusted road home. Not when he stared into the flaring eyes of the devil cat (or so the villagers believed the man-eater to be) and his trigger jammed. Not when looking at pitifully mauled bodies or when sitting over kills, waiting night long for a potential lethal leopard's return.

Those nights at the Black Rock taught me many things: to lose a fish is not the end of all and that acceptance is everything. It also showed to me finally that a hero of the ilk of Metha and Corbett I am not. Poor, puny me. Firstly I was beaten by the mahseer and secondly I had even to put down my copy of *The Man Eater of Rudraprayag*: every twig snapping, every grain of sand stirring spoke of my imminent and appalling end. Utter silence was even worse: a man-eater would never make a sound so soundlessness that it came to spell certain death! Every day was a climax at the Black Rock. Mahseer and passion are inextricably linked and the best and the worst was brought out in us all I believe. If good did come out of those days perhaps — as I've hinted — our film helped spark a rebirth of mahseer fishing in India. If mahseer are to exist long into this new century they need to be viewed by the Indians themselves as sport fish. There is a new India now, a land of progress and expanding horizons. It's not difficult to see that men like Corbett and Metha can be replaced by the wealthy, middle-class Indians from the cities who take delight in their jungle areas. It could well be that these new Indians will save stretches of mahseer river presently under threat simply by taking up their fishing rods. I hope so and pray so because mahseer are just too special to lose.

Paul Boote was — and is — built of sterner stuff, I guess. Through all our days together at the Black Rock and before during the weeks spent in Kashmir and northern India it was hard to fathom exactly what was going through the mind of this intense and private man. Paul went on to hunt one of the world's most savage freshwater fish, the Goliath tiger, in one of the world's most dangerous rivers, the Congo. I, on the other hand, decided that my mahseer fishing techniques so obviously needed to improve! Since Black Rock days, I've pulled my socks up and tangled with many a mahseer, frequently successfully because, I believe, those days on the Ganges did give me a focus I'd previously lacked. But, I still don't get it all, or much come to that. Certainly the biology of mahseer is way beyond me. What can I say? Gold mahseer are arguably the kings — or should it be queens. Scales like flowing gold that simply explode in the sunlight but, by a nose, I lean towards silvers. The scale colourings are slightly more subtle with a hint of pewter and even turquoise in bright light. But the tails...oh, those tails. It's no use describing them because I swear you will never have seen a blue to compare. An ecstatic violet is as close as I personally can get. Greens are marvellous too, rather like silvers but overlaid with a haze of silkiest seaweed you can ever imagine. Lovely. But blacks...now we're in the realms of fantasy. Out of three or four hundred mahseer I have seen or caught personally just two have been blacks and small ones both. Size though rarely matters and certainly not in this case: the blacks are like fish covered in lace but still with spectacularly orange fins, which are exotically enhanced by this coal-dusted body. Blacks — especially large ones — are now excruciatingly rare and when a few years ago I missed out on seeing a seventy-six pounder by a few minutes I realised this was an opportunity unlikely to be repeated.

I ought also to say something about the different shape strains of mahseer. In essence, Himalayan mahseer (Barbus Tor Puttitora) those living in the turbulent streams of the north, are generally considered to be slimmer than the more portly fish of the south, essentially of the River Cauvery. In fact, you could describe them as barbel rather than carp. The humpback fish of the south are frequently referred to as (Barbus Tor) Mussullah or Khudree or even Kolus. And on and on it goes — especially when good authority has it that the mahseer of Burma and Tibet all have their own eccentricities. To tell you the truth, I'm not even sure about the basic divisions of colour and I've made too many mistakes and been corrected on too many occasions to state anything with absolute certainty. In my mind, there's a degree of snobbery about the classification of the different types of mahseer and I instinctively shy away from any verdict. Be like me, perhaps: just be happy to catch a mahseer of any shape, size or colour if you get the chance. Catch them? Now there's a thing.

It was one of those mornings that I realised you can fish a lifetime away and not know much at all. Dawn. Western Nepal. We were rafting a tributary of the mighty Karnali river and the previous night camp had been struck on a beach at the head of a glide. The Boys — Gerry, Pasang and Kami — had sworn that they'd seen good mahseer here in the past and we turned in early, about 10.00 pm, full of good feelings. They were soon proved to be right. As the light grew the next day, the river smoked and appeared as a slithering sheet of silver. I began at the head of the long run, casting a plug across and down. Four casts, then three paces in classic Raj-mahseer fashion. Nothing, but I was at peace with the sunrise, when, quite unexpectedly, the river began to explode with mahseer. They were in the margins. They were in mid river. They were at the head of the pool, through its belly and out at the tail. I was looking at hundreds of yards of rolling mahseer. At times fifty fish were breaking surface simultaneously, perhaps more. Prey fish were sheering clear of the surface wherever you looked, pursued by relentless bow waves. The sound too was enough to wake the Boys and Joy from their slumbers...endless crashes as big fish launched themselves skywards. There were tails waving, caught by the now streaming sunlight. Backs showed over a metre long. Golden scales glittering. A sixty pounder nearly brushed my legs, mouth agape, vacuuming up the fleeing chilwa (the generic Indian term for small fish). The Boys sat on the bank cheering as mahseer hurtled themselves a body's length into the air. I could sense them congratulating each other for, they'd done it, they'd shown me mahseer paradise after so many days afloat.

Joy fumbled for her own rod and joined me. We cast until our arms dropped off, our backs groaned and our wrists felt mangled. We changed lures a dozen times or more and yet in just over an hour of the most frenzied, sustained predatorial behaviour I've ever witnessed, we didn't get as much as a pull. I'm not even convinced that we had a genuine follow. There must have been at least two hundred or more ravenous mahseer within our casting range for an hour and not a single hit. I've turned that day over and over in my mind ever since and even though I know how bewildering mahseer behaviour can be, it still makes no sense. You would have expected one fish at least to have made a single error of judgement. The whole episode remains a mystery to me. Once the sun was full on the river and the final plumes of mist spiralled away, all activity ceased as suddenly and completely as it had begun. The Boys stood hands on

hips. Joy and I looked at each other and waded slowly, disconsolately back to the bank. 'At least we're alive,' she said.

This was a trip Joy claimed had presented her with a hundred and seven brushes with death. Nonsense, of course. Professional travellers can be absurd. Our flight west from Kathmandu had, in truth, been so turbulent that even the pilots were passed the sick bags, but a brush with death? Hardly. And, yes, a leopard did come through our camp the second evening, calmly picking up a cockerel and merging off into the blackness with it. But it did grab the bird and not us. Nor can I accept that a hundred and three even less disturbing events really carried the threat of curtains for either of us. That leaves just two moments when I was truly concerned...

We heard the rapids half an hour or so before coming to them so we knew they were significant enough before we saw them surging in a wide arc under steep cliffs. Joy and I fished for perhaps an hour whilst the Boys went off to recce, a time long enough for us both to hook and lose good mahseer at the head of the white water. White were just what the Boys were on their return. None of us liked what was coming, naturally, but there was no way out but down and they lashed the raft, us, themselves, the luggage and the last remaining chicken together as if our lives depended on it. We put our head gear on and checked our lifejackets and half way around the bend I saw exactly what was coming to us: beneath stretched out what I can only describe as a ladder of white diving into a cauldron of foam. It didn't take us long to travel the ladder — about the length of a very deep gasp really — and the raft didn't capsize or overturn exactly either. Rather it reared up to the absolute vertical, teetered as if to flip and then crashed down. I was in the front, doing my best to force the snout back towards the water and turned round ecstatic with our triumph. There was no-one there. Even the hen had cleared off. The Boys joined me a couple of whirlpools later, hoisting themselves and a few recovered items of baggage aboard. Of Joy, there was not a sign. Her straw hat, a size four flip-flop, both floated past. For two minutes, slightly more perhaps, we held position in the slowing current, scanning the river, peering towards the rock crevasses on the far bank. When she did bob up five yards away from us it was with the force of a cork and in an instant Gerry had her by the scruff of her neck and she was coughing and slithering on the floor of the raft. Over the next twenty minutes we collected all the luggage we could find, pretty well near everything but for the chicken. Through all this, Joy sat in total quietness on the beach amongst the soaked clothing we'd spread out to dry. The Boys and I looked at her suspiciously, at each other meaningfully. It was a good hour after the accident when, quite out of the blue, she turned to us: 'Hope the hen made it. Perhaps she'll marry a jungle cock.'

The night after this we camped quarter of a mile or so beneath the small creek that we spied entering the main river — a sure mahseer hunting ground come the following dawn. Joy and I were up at cockcrow — if only we'd had one left — and pushed through the elephant grass that separated us from the creek entrance. Small packs of medium-sized mahseer drifted in and out of the current, harrying small carp and chilwa into the still water where they could make an easy kill. A Nepali materialised out of the mist, watched us catch a fourteen pounder before standing up and waving goodbye. He had gone perhaps ten paces when he paused, turned, pointed and called out a single word. 'Tiger.'

You learn to read people and their body language on journeys like this and Joy's face went from white to red to white again with a rapidity that alarmed me. 'You hear that, John? You hear what he said? Tiger? He meant a tiger in there. In there. My God. In there. I'm swimming back.' I looked at the torrent between us and the camp and shook my head. No way. The sensible thing would have been to fish on, waited for the Boys to awake and get them to come for us. Strength lies in numbers but not for Joy, off into the elephant grass

following the track back to the camp. Holding the rod before us, I took the lead and halfway in I realised the man had been correct. Ahead, great spoor marks decorated the mud, slowly filling with water. On or back? No time for a decision. The grasses to our left began to switch evermore violently and then She burst through, a vast, tawny tigress, an animal of burnished gold, a sight so stunning the world stopped turning. She reared up almost at the rod tips, clawed at the air with a paw the size of a tennis racket. All the while the rumble in her chest rose to a full, ear shattering roar. Her teeth. Her tongue. Her eyes. Her smell on the dank air. Did this last for five seconds or five minutes? I don't know. I still believe Joy slid down my left side into the grass. She thinks not. It doesn't matter: what does is that the tigress was gone, the bending grasses marking her way.

Back at camp, the Boys were waiting for us, ashen once more. A brush with death, we asked? 'Only dangerous if she'd been with cubs, Joy,' said Pasang. 'Or perhaps if one of you had run,' added Gerry. 'Or then again, if she'd just been feeling mean,' put in Kami as a last word.

There are times — did-the-earth-move-for-you-times — when you know a particular fish is beyond your own capabilities to land. Part of this is physical. Your gear simply isn't up to the job; your experience and technique are both found wanting and in tatters. Even if you hang on, and miraculously the fish is still attached, you're gone in your mind, whacked mentally. All you can do is call out for help and hope a presence emerges skilful and sensitive, able to guide you through the tempest. Tempest I hear you say? What is going on? We're talking about a fish, simply a fish. Okay but it can be a fish that means the absolute world and remember that's how fishing can become at its most extreme limits. There are some fish that mean so desperately much and sometimes I wonder whether all fish shouldn't do that to you. Why else should you want to put a hook in them unless it's something you feel really compelled to do . . . .

I saw Simon talk Phil through the landing of his huge taimen on a day when the Siberian winds were blowing and the raft that they were fighting the fish from was half sinking. Even through binoculars, it was quite obvious that Phil's legs had turned to jelly and that Simon was the metaphorical rock on which he was leaning. I believe Phil would be the first to admit that he wouldn't have stood a chance of landing that fish on his own, no more than I would have done on the Cauvery back in 1990 when I hit into a large mahseer on Broken Rod Pool. Broken Rod Pool — there's a relevant story to

that one. Two weeks previously I'd had a rod snap on me as I tried to hold a mahseer tight there and keep it from the rapids beneath. The rod had gone off like a pistol shot just above the butt, a bullet in the heart of the whole enterprise. You don't often get second chances in life and now Subhan said we'd have to do something different if lightning were to strike twice. Understand landing a mahseer is as big a problem as hooking them in the first place, for the fight is at least as great as its reputation. You've only got to look at a mahseer to understand why: the fins, especially the under-body fins are just gigantic. Those pectorals, that amazing anal fin. But no, they all are: the dorsal is extraordinary and as for the tail... they're truly all like walls of muscle.

Back to Broken Rod and for a while we looked safe: I'd worked the pool itself with a big silver spoon and guessed that the pod of fish had moved on. It was a blindingly hot day and I was feeling distinctly edgy, having no real desire to hook up again in such a perilous pool. But no, it wasn't set to be a gentle afternoon. As so often happens, right at the tail of the pool where the water begins to break up amongst rocks a big fish took in the streaming current. I saw the sun winking on the spoon as it came back towards me and then a shadow emerged behind and then the heart-lurching hammer of the take. Only a second of real time but it's imprinted on your memory for eternity. Subhan, lounging beneath a tree, burst into life. 'Pump, sah. Pump. Pump, bloody well pump.'

'But I can't. I can't hold it. It's going down. It's...'

No need, no time for more words. From the lip of the white water a golden shape emerged, tail slapping defiantly and then it was gone, leaving me with a fast-emptying spool of angling tradition. Subhan drew himself to his full height, kicked off his flip-flops, looked at me steely-eyed and said, 'We swim, sah. Now, bloody hell, we swim sah.' Two years ago, the first time I had returned, I paced that crazy mahseer chase from point of entry to final, exhausted exit... nine

hundred and thirty yards of water volcanic with rocks and white-crested waves. Twice the mahseer snagged, on a rock the first time and a log the second: each time, Subhan dived, located the problem, broke the line below the obstruction and above the fish and retied it at the rod tip. He was nothing but a blob of brown sucked into the foaming white of a river raging like a bull elephant, where all I could do was tread water, look for sanctuary and pray. I guess it was half an hour before the three of us – fish, guide and fisherman – floundered into the calm of the pool beneath and we were all done for. It should have been a formality to reel in the exhausted mahseer but I could barely turn the reel handle, Subhan was a drowned otter and it was a further ten minutes before he called for the stringer rope to pass through the gills of what remains one of my biggest mahseer captures.

Despite the big reputations that have been made out in Southern India, I hardly think a single fish would be landed from the Cauvery without the presence of Subhan, Bola, Krea, KN or any one of those guides whose knowledge of the river and the fish is so immense. There's a lot of macho crap that goes on there and many a toast drunk to an angler that wouldn't come within a million miles of his mahseer if he'd been fishing on his own. Courage, determination

and cool-headed calculation are bred into these guides. And women come to that. Over and over, the English angler had bragged about his big fish.

'Have you ever seen one like it, Bola?'

'Yes, sah.' A pause. 'My mother, sah, she land a hundred and twelve pounder. On a hand line. Four hours fight, sah. She lost a finger. Real big fish, real fisherman, sah. Yes, real fisherman.'

Obviously, making dreams come true for Westerners who only debatably deserve them has its rewards. These guide are the gods of their valley with their passed-on designer tee shirts, baseball caps, big dollar tips and ricochets of reflected affluence. Mahseer have been good to them and their families and given them a status they could never have found in any other way of life. Rather like the Sherpas in the Himalayas, the Cauvery fishing guides rightly enjoy their own personal stardoms. Guiding offers a lifestyle that these men are anxious to protect, of course, and so stretches of the River Cauvery are fought for like no other watercourses in India. Here we have an example of how sport fishing can work to the benefit of all, even to the fish themselves. I'd never say mahseer enjoy the experience of being caught — certainly not when you consider how hard they fight to avoid it — but it's probably preferable to being dynamited and there's an added, spooky postscript.

Once the fish have been subdued and the stringer has been threaded through their gill flaps, they become totally changed creatures. If you wade out into the shallows close to them the chances are that they will swim towards you, brush past you, drift between your legs and allow themselves, sometimes, even to be stroked. I do not know if it's a case of their wills being broken, of an obeisance to a superior force but I've always seen it as less demeaning than that. My sense has been of a more fundamental and even spiritual experience, a kind of bonding between fisher and fish. Remember, if you can, that fight back in the school playground and how your adversary suddenly became your best friend and, somehow, the experience feels the same under the heat of the Indian sun. You've tested and tried each other and the contest was so close that the result hardly matters in the end. Nonsense? Perhaps, but then little in India is how it superficially seems and if you think it is, you're missing out on layer upon layer of experience. And if you really don't get that, you possibly shouldn't be there in the first place. So much of what's going on isn't the pretty postcard stuff you might well think it is initially. In a single hour you are likely to see disease, cases of malnutrition, a leper in the street and a broken-legged beggar child. You'll be pursued by the skeletal-faced woman with the rag baby. You might smell your first corpse, burning on a pyre and if it's not that it will be the smell of sewage in a stinking backwater that fills your nostrils. And all this is happening in an atmosphere of disregard that first of all you believe is callous but is actually one of acceptance. When you're in India you build a shell around yourself, not one that's really protective but one that's more a realisation of how life is in the real world. Cushioned as we are in the West, a trip to India is well worth making if only to let the whiff of mortality into our nostrils and never again do you complain that the 8.10 into work is running a few minutes overdue.

There was (or is) one form of mahseer that had always eluded me, as everybody else. The chocolate mahseer is a fish that hasn't been seen, as far as I know, for nigh on a hundred years. It began to appear, in the mid nineteen nineties, that the only place where any chance of chocolates still existing would be somewhere in the extreme boundaries of Arunachal Pradesh, a tiny area sandwiched into the apex between Tibet to the west, China to the north and Burma to the east. I might as well tell you that I've agonised over writing this last piece on the sub-continent: it's not as though nothing happened, it certainly did, but even with the help of my expedition diary everything seems to have taken on a dream-like

sequence since. Perhaps that's an exaggeration: probably what I'm trying to say is that I find it very difficult to get any significant focus on that journey. I have no perspective on it, no way of knowing whether it were a success or a failure — though I guess just coming back with the team intact was success enough. Also, we did find the river we were searching and we did catch something — but more of that to come.

Possibly one of my problems with the trip is that I felt totally out of control, lost and disoriented. Half the time I was just wondering where the hell I'd brought us all to and realised I was relying solely on John Edwards and his team. What I do remember is the seemingly endless journey into the Yamne valley, a trek of hours, no days, vivid but hopelessly jumbled. From Calcutta we took a plane to a landing strip in nowhere. Then it was a large ferry up the Brahmaputra river in a glowing sunset. I remember that well: the falling sun looked impossibly large and painted us all coppery as we drank our Kingfisher beers. We were excited to be on the great river, over a mile wide, endlessly deep, effortlessly strong, from time to time serenaded by the graceful roll of a freshwater dolphin.

Darkness. A Dervish jeep ride thorough black jungle. Once we were ferried over a stream in the pitch darkness and several times we had to stop to clear rocks from the track in front of us. Very occasionally the lamps from settlements glowed momentarily and then were lost. Even less frequently a figure would appear in our headlights, perhaps driving a lonely cow home. What remained of the night we spent in a 'roach-ridden bungalow in some far-flung, near-forgotten settlement. Daylight again and it was onwards towards the north: more ferries, more tracks ever narrowing. Ravines ever deepening, mountains ever more massive. I do remember very clearly a swing bridge over the river, made from ancient bamboo slats many of which broke away and helicoptered down into the dizzying space beneath my boot. The Bridge of Death

I recalled from some half-forgotten Monty Python film. I was afraid. So afraid I believed I could not go on but I knew, equally, that I could not go back. I wondered why the blowing wind didn't turn the bridge turtle and catapult me off into the void? Whether the handrail, knee height there, could ever save me? At the far end, slumped exhausted into the undergrowth: within half an hour I'd watched two village men crossing the bridge, one playing a guitar, the second with a calf slung across his shoulders! We came to a ravine down to the camp, so impossibly steep that even John stumbled, fell and we all held our breaths. In the pit of the valley the shadows entombed us and the sky was a distant patch of blue, swallowed up by the jungle. We collapsed, thoroughly exhausted, into our tents.

John Edwards had 'sold' me the idea a six-month lifetime before our departure date: it's so easy to say yes to something that will never happen, to be seduced by a map not poured over by a European for nigh on a century. I remember his voice that night. The wine. The music. You know how it is...'An exclusion zone set up by the government back in the twenties. No English, no Indians, no-one for seventy-five years. A forbidden paradise. But my wife, as you know, is a princess of the people. So perhaps... perhaps there is still a chocolate mahseer there, John. Yes, chocolate. Last caught, I believe in that region. Possibly in the very place I'm aiming for. Back in 1907. Of course I don't know what they look like. Does anyone who is still alive? A safe journey? What is safe, John? Who knows the answer to that one?' And because I trust John Edwards more than anyone else with my life and because I knew it would never come to pass, I promised to put together a team.

I would have applied the same persuasion techniques if I'd had to: the yellowing map, faded photographs, promises of piscatorial immortality but I didn't have to. Not remotely. Not with a guy like Keith Elliott absorbed in the history of angling. Not with somebody like Simon Channing, an obsessed adventurer always looking to push

the limits. Not with Dave Wilson, like me on the cusp of middle age and perhaps with things to prove.

'What are trumps?' It's easy enough for me to see us all there now, at night, sitting round the table washed by the glow of the paraffin lamps. Cards. Two bottles of Johnnie Walker, one empty, the second disappearing fast. Keith all mischievous goblin, John playing the card sharp. Dave and I eternally bemused and Simon, young, naïve and winning every hand. Every girl's heart.

I'd better deal with the fishing first to placate the angler in you. It's become near an apocryphal story, hasn't it? Every trip to India has to have its monster break free as though you're not a man until you've been mashed by a mahseer. This time it was John who was destroyed. He hooked a big fish up river of me the first night and I heard his cries. More importantly, I saw the fish come down the rapids that separated us: it was, I guess, some ten yards away from me and perhaps a hundred downriver of John. I could see at that point that there was no chance of him landing it. Even if he'd gone into the river the fish had made too much ground to be caught and I believed as it went past me it had already broken free. Big? Yes, very. That sadly was our only big fish: we'd come all that way and we were just too late. The mahseer that had left the mighty Brahmaputra for the only slightly smaller Siang and then come to spawn up the Yamne had been and they'd gone and the window of opportunity was shut firmly in our faces by the tail of that last, big, fleeing fish. That's how it can be so easily and we had no alternative but to accept what nature decreed. But a chocolate? Well. We think, perhaps...I have a photograph in my collection of something that looks very much like a mahseer and is certainly exactly the colour of chocolate, albeit a murky, milk brand. So, if you put the shape and the colouring together, then, yes, we all agreed we'd either done it or at least come close. But, in our hearts, I guess none of us is absolutely sure. The fish was a juvenile, around about four pounds in weight and I have to say, in all honesty, that it could easily have belonged to a branch of the carp family I haven't previously met up with. We celebrated sure, but in a guarded fashion as though we all had doubts we weren't overly keen to express to each other. We'd come a long way, we'd given of our best and we weren't in the mood to pass up on any straws.

Never has the old adage been truer that you've got to sniff the roses on the way than during this particular journey. We were based close to a village and I think we'd all agree that it was the most remarkable place any of us have ever visited. Remember that we really were treading back in time, that the clock had been broken back in the nineteen twenties by that exclusion zone and the hands had hardly moved on since. We were the first Europeans that all but the oldest inhabitants in the valley had ever seen. They were in awe of our cameras, binoculars, fishing tackle and, above all, Walkmans! After the amazement seeped away, the laughter settled in: they wanted to know why we were pink and not white. How come our feet were so abnormally large? And why were we so hairy...were we related to the apes? The men fingered our blond hair whilst the women examined the texture of our clothing and the children played with our presents of pens and balloons. No coke cans there, baseball caps or plastic flip-flops — the usual detritus of a Third World village. No, just proud, untrammelled, unalloyed beauty.

Perhaps it's here that I'm going off the rails. Perhaps even my journal, made day to day, is mistaken but I still remember that place as some sort of paradise, the Shangri-La that beckons every traveller onwards. There can be no doubt that the village in its valley setting was extraordinarily beautiful: the forest-clad cliffs, the achingly beautiful Yamne river and the paddy fields and orchards all shimmered in the rarest, clearest of lights. It is possibly these colours, so delicate and clean, that I remember the clearest. It was like being in a world newly rinsed with not a single stain on its purity. The girls danced for us and they were, as you knew I'd say,

extraordinarily beautiful. They wore necklaces of Victorian rupees and moved with exquisite grace. The village elders told us that here there was no theft, no such thing as a lock or a key. All were equal, men, women and children though the tradition of ancestor worship meant that some of the older men were endowed with a special dignity and given the lead in decision making. The climate, they agreed, was perfect. Even in the monsoons, you could expect no more than two or three hours rain a day and winters were benign. Though there were still tigers in the forests around, these played an important economic function: any animal hunted could be traded with the next village down river for essential items like ammunition or...in fact they needed little else.

The tall man wearing the bearskin hat spoke. He said that we were obviously people from a much more developed civilisation and asked us how he could improve the life of his tribe. We looked around at the contentment, the cleanliness and the beauty and were lost for words. Especially so when our interpreter told us that there was no word in this man's language for stress, worry or anxiety. I said, 'Tell him to forget we've ever been to this place. Wash us from your memory.'
1ST NOVEMBER

This does seem like a dream to me now and perhaps my vagueness is something to do with the amount of chung that I'd drunk during the course of the day. Chung is the evil product of par-boiled rice and yeast which is left to ferment. There's a great skill to making this drink and according to the 'hand' that stirs it, generally a lady's, it will taste either sweet or sour. Certainly, the chung that I'd drunk that day was sweet, refreshing and hugely alcoholic. At one point, an ancient warrior came to greet us, regaled in all his fighting finery. He sported a huge headdress, necklaces of tiger teeth and claws and brandished a mighty-looking spear. We were, after all, on the fringes of head-hunters' territory where certainly up until a handful of years

before raids had been made for these cherished symbols of omnipotent manhood. And no word for stress in their language ...

We pulled out of camp on 4th November and left the Yamne valley with heavy hearts feeling deep down we would never make a return. What we didn't know was that the journey back to Calcutta would involve us in alarms and excursions way beyond what any of us were expecting. A raft that nearly sank and a dilapidated taxi that crashed off the road, through a hut and into the midst of a family dinner, were only a part of it. Only when we were sitting in a BA flight bound for London did Keith think it safe enough to order champagne. And, of course, get out the cards.

CHAPTER
6

THE TURNING
OF THE TIDE

'No horizons, no islands, no shade from the burning sun.
We moved like gunslingers through the shin-deep water and
then, after more than an hour of walking, Fidel pointed to the
biggest shoal of bonefish that has ever been seen, I guess, in
the history of the world!'

ONE PERSON IN A THOUSAND who looks out on the seashore fully understands it. No, far, far less than that and certainly not I who came too late to the coast to graft it onto my soul, let salt run in my veins. I might have only been ten or so when my parents bought a house whose windows could be rattled by winter storms but the time had passed for me. The North Norfolk Coast is a nebulous place where the shore mingles with the sea and the line between is desperately hard to draw especially in a mist or in a storm when the jealous sea rages to take back space lost to it. The old boys used to say that there's nothing between the North Pole and us and I'd half expect a white bear to ride in on the rollers. Wide-eyed with wonder, I threw myself into this world of greys and greens, catching crabs from the village quayside, eels from the endless dykes, mackerel from the shingle banks that were constructed to keep the sea out of all our living rooms. Sometimes they did. Sometimes not. Winters can be savage here and when freezing north and north-westerlies blow for any amount of time terrible events occur. There's cold so intense that birds are frozen in the marshes. Worst still, the waters of the northern oceans are heaped up against the low-lying Norfolk shoreline, forced into the southern North Sea and funnelled between the coasts of England and Europe. There is only one

narrow, insufficient exit for these countless tons of water, the twenty-one mile gap between Dover and Calais. The huge force of water cannot escape anywhere quickly enough and the seas accumulate and rise, pushing back relentlessly towards this fragile coastline. If the gales coincide with a high spring tide then the likely outcome is disaster. The modern term is a tidal surge: the old men of the village know these periodic inundations as Rages. How apt: sleet, spray, an unstoppable tide, a wicked display of almighty ill temper. Farmland destroyed, sea walls swept away. Cottages helpless against the flood. Inevitable loss of life.

I've experienced Rages, but never the truly awful ones that occur every half century or so and either change, or take your life. So even in this respect I've never quite become one with this unique environment, the total man of the seashore. Even though for a while I made my living from it and as it happens, very nearly my dying.

In those days, and we're talking a quarter of a century back, lugworm digging was a staple industry of the tiny villages hereabouts. The worms were sold to long liners off Yarmouth or to London anglers hiring a boat off the Essex ports. Cod were still kings, great, fat, creamy fish raiding the eastern coastline for its rich pickings from autumn through to spring. I had been working, post college, on a farm in the sprout shed with some forty or so women and they were running me round as a barrel. I felt like I was living in some Thomas Hardy novel where all was flirtation and innuendo and snatched kisses here and there in the darkened winter farmyard.

Joe and Bernie rescued me though, true seashore men who could sense the mood of the tide, feel the shift of the sands and hear the wandering of the crabs but even they could and did get things wrong. Where the sky, the sea and the shadowy shore merge there's an elasticity and a blurring of boundaries that can make anyone, even them, lose their focus. It is so long ago, I can barely remember how the day was before the terror set in. I know that we were digging

127

along the Wash, that bite out of the eastern English coastline where the tides seep in and out so seductively that many before us have been betrayed. It was there that King John lost his fabled treasure to the seas eight hundred years ago and we all dug deep, half expecting to unearth a crown or a diamond-encrusted sword. We were going flat out to fill a big order and I remember vaguely a bright day turning to mist and a breeze subsiding to nothing. Joe's singsong voice called out to dig the last hundred worms and then, quite suddenly, there was water in my trench, water everywhere sliding across the sands. The smiles froze on our faces and we turned to run before the sea. But where? Our footsteps out from the land had melted. The fog had draped the whole world under a grey curtain until the shoreline and the sea's horizon truly were one. Nor was there even a wind now to guide us home and the direction of the incoming water, that we knew could never be trusted, followed its own crazy patterns up the gulleys and down the channels. I suppose it would have been Joe who made the decision on direction and we took off after him, hearts beating, mouths dry. About to die? No, not here I felt. Not now. I still couldn't quite take it seriously and I guess I must have trotted after Joe like some spaniel only increasingly struck by the silence and by the menace of the rising water. No, for once, there was no talking and joking as we walked off the sands that day, just grim determination, lengthening strides, the splash of water at our shins, our knees and eventually our thighs. I couldn't begin to tell you how far we followed Joe that afternoon, how close we were to death but I do know we had never been happier to see the dark green smudge of the foreshore and to throw our heaving, racked bodies up onto the beds of lavender. And then, like young men do, we got up and got on with our lives.

There was a diggers' brotherhood, a do-and-die mentality, an all-for-one philosophy. Cawcaw, Sykes, Percy, Ching... nearly everyone had their nickname though why mine was Bingo I'll never quite understand. We all played football together on Saturday afternoons and during the rest of the week, if we weren't digging, then we were fishing. I remember now wild winter nights shore fishing for cod by the light of a Tilley lamp, 'It's a whacker,' Billy said, looking at me and Joe. 'We can cut it into three halves and we'll all have a good feed.' Or we'd go pike fishing on hard-frozen Sunday mornings. We'd drive in excitement along the track through the wood and up the steep hill to the bailiff's cottage to buy our tickets, all because we might stand a chance of seeing his pale but astoundingly beautiful daughter looking at us from behind a twitched curtain. Cruelly, we'd persuaded him his woods were full of aardvark and he became a laughing stock at the next county fair, poor man. Sometimes we speared flatfish in the pools left by the ebb or tried to net shoals of mullet as they explored the creek on the flow. Could we, though, stop them leaping over the top like so many disappearing greyhounds? Only by placing a second net beneath the first, so close that they couldn't pace themselves for an ensuing leap, could we hope to pick up more than one or two fish. We had a boat that we'd take ten miles or so offshore, and use fresh caught mackerel as bait for tope that screamed line off in those shallow, warm seas. We poached Zeterman's carp pond. When we were caught, Percy pretended I was his idiot brother and we got away with it until the Zetermans themselves appeared at one of my parents' cocktail parties. Best of all we netted the shore for bass, always at night and generally after a good, heavy blow. One of us would row in a large arc, paying out the net whilst the others held the end and pulled it back at the completion of each manoeuvre. Exciting stuff and you'd feel the bass hit the meshes and, if the sea were calm and the moon was big, you'd even see the corks pulled under and splashy boils heave on the surface.

This is more than a nostalgic lament for a lost world of boyhood: I suppose I'm trying to make some kind of statement. In a mere

quarter of a century, the lugworms have all but gone and only one of the old team, Ching, still hacks a living from them. The kids wouldn't dream of going out there, suffering the winter's cold on their backs and the salt water deep in their blisters. Not that the worms are there anymore, their beds destroyed by insidious pollution. The cod, too, are a memory and everyone knows here that over fishing is responsible for that. Mullet and bass still visit in reduced numbers but of the last, still unmentioned summer nomad, there remains hardly any trace. I'm talking about sea trout and from time to time we would catch one in our nets, generally fish of three to five pounds but occasional monsters over twelve pounds. Cawcaw told me that they made their way up the two short rivers and I was soon to experience the most exciting night of my fishing life. It was Cawcaw too that had spotted the group of fish earlier that day on the big bend just below the old bridge by the church. Though it was early June, the weather was red raw, as it often can be when the wind comes in from the north. Low cloud draped the entire valley in a drizzling mist but as evening pulled in I was determined to get out there before the fish should leave.

I stood on the bridge looking out but the light was too low to see anything in the water. But, fate! A splash beneath the willow, no, a huge roar like a boy falling in. It was obscene in the way that it ripped the silence apart. I settled in quickly amongst the high wet grasses and put out a line. The flies skated across the surface, making a slight 'v'. The water around it seemed to well and the log of a head appeared. The line snapped tight and without quite knowing how, I was off after a great fish cartwheeling silver in the gloom. Sometimes the fish sulked, head in the weed, tail strumming the current but generally the surge back towards the safety of the sea continued inexorably, exhaustingly, a strain on my body, a nightmare for my nerves. I've always felt, even as a kid, that if you suffer a fish the indignity of putting a hook in its mouth, at the very least you must want to land it so much you'd die if you don't ... and I've never felt that more strongly before or since that night. Just sometimes a ray of hope entered my heart — surely that last run was less strong than the ones before — that leap was more a flop, a tired cry for help. But then, inevitably despair would take over once more as the rod hammered back, the reel gave more and more line, the backing ever lower on the spool.

And then, after an age, I saw the bridge, the bridge of doom with its sluice gates to the sea and freedom. For over ten minutes that last eighty yards was fought out between us. I was losing the battle, I knew, like a climber whose fingertips slide down the rock face to eternal darkness. The fish smelled the sea and the salt pumped in its veins. The sluice gate was life and how was a gossamer line like mine going to stop such a fish from living it? The final play was acted in slow time, right there in the shadows of the bridge, a whirlpool of swirls, a volley of leaping. Then came the grating, the sudden slackness and my heart melted like a snowflake in the sea. I was aware that an old boy had been watching the final drama and as I wound in my fifty yards of slack line, he cycled away with a shake of his head. No doubt to the pub, to tell them that the young lad hadn't been up to it. I hated that: in those days, The Bell was the centre of my little universe where I felt I had so much to prove. And now I'd failed. But most of all I hated the loss of that fish: it was like a pain, a real hurt, an ache so real it's hard to describe to those who haven't been there. I got myself washed up, I remember and drove up to The Bell. I pushed open the door and there was a perceptible pause before I was swamped with offers for a drink. Denny had reported back all right but I'd become a mini local hero. 'Bloody hard luck, Bingo boy,' called out Sykes. And when Carol, too, from behind the bar called out her condolences well ... I was just on top of the world.

Recently Christopher and Maddie took a job on the most remote of Scottish western isles — they wouldn't appreciate me telling you

131

which — and I guess a major reason for their move was the other-worldly sea trout fishing they'd located there. Hard to explain, this sea trout thing but you know when you've got it. Drives men mad, out onto the river night after night, or down to Tierra del Fuego or Sweden or anywhere there's a chance of a special fish. This is why Christopher is on his island because here you can catch them from the seashore itself, without waiting for them to climb a river. Sea trout from the seashore on a fly rod. An easy decision. Three planes and a ferry later and they were waiting for me, man and dog at the harbour.

June. The perfect month, my journey timed to coincide with the newest of moons so the nights would be as dark as they can get at this latitude. We left my bags at the cottage and walked to the shore, Maddie bounding away in the surf, great brown ears parachuting behind him under the force of the wind. Christopher pointed to a place where channels crisscrossed, creating a maze of inlets and islands. 'This is the place. As the tide comes and goes, these gulleys become racing salt rivers. The sea trout flood in.' His eyes glistened. 'It's the best, it's magic.'

We spent the afternoon putting up tackle and from the early evening we drank red wine whilst Christopher prepared a cold sea trout salad ready for our return the coming dawn. 'The tide will be high around eleven so that's when we will be there. It's not the incoming tide that works here but the ebb. Don't ask me why. Nothing makes sense up here but it means the best of it will be from midnight till around two or three at the latest I guess. Chest waders, yes. A lifejacket is sensible, I suppose. A torch if you must. And a whistle.' Maddie looked up as we put on our boots, his tail thumping the tiles, a bark of excitement in his throat.

There was thick cloud above and it was dark as pitch. And silent. No noise you'd think but then I noticed the murmur of the sea beyond the islands and the lapwings calling in the shallow dunes behind. Enjoying the swoosh of the line through the air. Treading carefully. Watching the rings of phosphorescence radiate out like a milky way at your feet. Like the stars of the sky are laid out on the sea. Aware now of lots of sounds. A dog or a fox perhaps barking. Far off sheep flocks. Maddie scuffling on the shore behind me, turning rocks over to look for crabs. Oh wow. This is it. It's what Christopher talked about...

Ten yards away the thin water was breaking into needles. Heavy splashes followed. A shoal of sea trout was chasing sand eels, the fish around my very feet. From somewhere close I heard Christopher's reel screaming on and on incessantly. Maddie was barking now, splashing towards us. Cast. Retrieve. Keep calm. Slow down my beating heart. Let me not die on a blissful night like this. My own line takes on a life and the rod becomes a twisting serpent in my hands. When Christopher called out triumphant in the blackness, 'Well, Johnny, happy are we? Worth coming all this way to the dark side of the moon?' Happy, like Maddie I'm ecstatic enough for my eyeballs to pop.

Fidel didn't think much of us — me, Magnus and Roger, all forty something, unattached males. 'None of you is married then? And no kids? Not one? Man! Do you want to share a bedroom or something? Is a poor boy like me safe with guys like you?' We explained. Angling adventurers. The fear of domestic ties. Responsibility and all that sort of thing. 'Kids ain't no tie, man,' Fidel explained for us. 'A few boxes of Pampers and away you go. I've six kids...'

'Seven,' Elvis interrupted.

'Seven kids and I love them all to bits and pieces. Bits and pieces. But I have a life, man. It ain't over for me yet.'

We'd guessed at that when Fidel had driven us from the island airport and we'd sat in the back of the pick-up on three white plastic chairs, feeling and probably looking like carnival queens. I'll rephrase that if you like but the point is every maiden we passed on the forty-minute journey fell into swoons at the sight of Fidel.

I was uneasy that first night on Acklin's, the last but one of the Bahaman islands. Perhaps it was the violent storm that lashed us, quivering the frail electrical supply, bouncing hail off the tin roof. True, the weather did make Acklin's feel more remote, alien even, but it was the easy calm in the eyes of Fidel and Elvis as they surveyed us that I found more unnerving than the weather or the place. Behind the joking, I could sense that we were being watched, surveyed, considered. Were we up for it? Up to it? Those eyes used to watching for bonefish, the ghosts of the flats, could see through us more easily than the clearest of water. Life on Acklin's has always been tough: just how soft were we? It was a look shared by Amos — Fidel's seventy-year-old father with the four-year-old daughter — and even Barbara, the lodge's cook. There'd be proving to do, I realised: I just wished it didn't have to be with bone fish, creatures of such staggering reputation that the three of us half felt defeated already. There was no bone fishing really until the end of the Second World War when the Americans gradually realised that these stunningly beautiful, quicksilver fish could be taken on the fly. Knowledge was hard won. Lefty Kreh proved to be a genius and partly because of him and largely because of the talented guides of the Caribbean and the Bahamas, bone fishing became the cult art form that it is today. Amos told us slowly that Elvis and Fidel had been taught by God to see bones and made us feel that we were here hanging onto the coat tails of all those gone before.

What I've got now is a series of images, not all of them comfortable ones. One is of the five of us — three fishermen and two guides — fanning out over a flat, seemingly as big as the world. It was endless.

No horizons, no islands, no shade from the burning sun. We moved like gunslingers through the shin-deep water and then, after more than an hour of walking, Fidel pointed to the biggest shoal of bonefish that has ever been seen, I guess, in the history of the world! There were hundreds and hundreds of bonefish before us, a swarming city of fish magicked out of the sea by Fidel. And then one of us — perhaps all three of us — put down bad casts and the flat erupted as wave upon wave of bones fled past in panic. I watched Fidel's eyes as they sought those of Elvis. Their eyes locked and spoke. The word was contempt.

Better was Copper Bottom, a wonderfully beautiful flat that you fish along westwards as the sun is sinking, spilling golden light in a glowing carpet before you. Pulse after pulse of bones worked towards us, groups of thirty to fifty fish in a seemingly endless procession. By now, by day three, we could all make out the nervous water that marked each grouping. Nervous water you can't describe any more by word than explaining blue to a blind man: you simply scan the flat and your eye picks out an area that doesn't somehow behave properly. If the surface is choppy, then nervous water is calm: if the flat is calm, nervous water is ruffled. Sort of. Focus on it, though, and you'll lose it altogether. Try to explain it as many have as a kind of static in the ripple pattern and you miss the essential truth of nervous water altogether. Nervous water is a sixth sense assuming a

tangible form. But, anyhow, we all caught fish that night from Copper Bottom and the light in the eyes was more friendly as we drank our beers and messed around on the pool table.

Best were the mangroves on the way to Lovely Bay where we all spotted bones finning over the bleached white sands, where Fidel approached them like a spirit, put out a long line on a whisper and hooked, fought and beached a big bone with masterly precision. We applauded and those eyes beamed out something that could have been warmth. No, I was misreading them, flattering myself. The truth is, neither Elvis nor Fidel ever exactly taught us anything. Yes, they pointed out fish to us until we understood a little of what we were looking for: nervous water of course and finning but also the deeper channels, depressions on the marl flats and the bare patches amongst the turtle grass. We picked up for ourselves that over marl, bones appear white, whilst atop turtle grass they sparkle like blue-green glass. We realised that the thousands of tiny mirror scales reflect the bones backdrop, painting them in eternal camouflage. We also learned how close to a group of fish to cast, how to twitch the fly at the right moment – and, importantly – how to give line under the correct pressure. All these things Elvis and Fidel were happy to help with, praise even, but I at least never got to the guts of the thing at all. Although I asked why the fish were here and not there, I was never answered. The key to any understanding is knowledge of the fish and this is what neither guide would ever give me. These were the bones belonging to Fidel and Elvis – not me. I'd have to find out for myself why they'd follow some tides and not others, why a wind could turn back thousands of fish and why some flats, seemingly perfect, rarely saw a single shoal. They were right. I didn't deserve to know all their sensitive secrets, magic they'd spent a lifetime learning. Though Magnus stayed on many more weeks, I don't believe they told him either. In fact, I don't think it was a particularly happy time for him: in trying to force some kind of acceptance of

rules white guys play to, he pushed them even further away from him. I dread to think what the eyes spoke by the time Fidel drove Magnus to the airstrip for that last time.

About things other than the lifestyle of bones, Elvis and Fidel would talk happily all night. For instance, they explained why even a four pound fish could break a ten pound leader if you tried to stop it in its tracks. 'Man, those bones can travel at twenty-six miles an hour. Twenty-six miles an hour. Can you believe that of a little old fish, man? That's why leaders go bust and that's why you've just got to let 'em go. Even if it means bringing them back two hundred yards afterwards.'

In general, life on Acklin's was about as laid back as any you'll find anywhere. Eternal friendships, barely any crime, ancient decayed walls dating back to the plantations and the slave forts all mark Acklin's as a world apart. A world as old as the wrecks of pirate ships off Lovely Bay with rusty anchors beneath where the crawfish hide. An island of six hundred people, mostly kids because the adults grow up and leave for the capital to the north. Girls have to be 'friendly' with both of them. There simply aren't enough girls left on Acklin's

as they all hanker for the lights of Nassau. Perhaps you can't blame them for wanting to leave this strange, scrub countryside behind them. What do young, pretty girls need with sugar cane, oranges, bananas, papaya, pigeon peas, Five Finger Trees, Strong Bark Trees and Horse Flesh Bushes? 'Black-top roads there ain't man,' said Elvis. 'Hell, after a rain, there ain't no tops anywhere anymore.'

Sitting there in a bar with Fidel and Elvis, watching the night sky, listening to the sea it was easy to hear voices of the past. Other bars and other places but the same stories of the land and the ocean. That's one thing Elvis and Fidel had, the closeness with their world that I'd experienced myself as a child. Sometimes they showed interest when I told them of my seashore, of how mullet looked not unlike bones and in some ways lived the same kind of lives in skinny water and turning tides. I told them my favourite stories from England, of the great storms from the past that men called the time of the Rages...

'Tell; that one of the big fish, man. That big, ole fish that your grandpapa cooked and ate...' Typically, Elvis didn't quite get the history right but the power of the tale affected us both. I settled down. 'It was New Year's Day around 1779.' Elvis looked doubtful. 'Two hundred years ago anyway. Around midnight a great gale sprang up blowing from the northwest, the worst direction for my village. It was high tide too and the water smashed the floodwall, swept over the marshes and hit the houses like a hammer. A big ship was carried on the flood and smashed down a complete house. Roofs were blown off in the wind and the tower of the church began to crumble. Men got into rowboats to try to escape to higher land. There were drowned cattle floating in the streets after they'd been washed from their barns. Boats in the harbour were sunk and there were bodies and barrels, masts and sails blowing against the walls of the cottages and the warehouses.' I look round. The beers were untouched. I had my audience. 'Then, like a switch, with the coming of the light, the storm eased and stopped. The sky was blue, the moon hung tattered and clear. Villagers assembled and looked over the now calm waters and the scenes of devastation. And then the worst thing. Almost by their feet, in the deep water by the quay side a huge fish rose up. It flung itself out of the sea showing its massive scaly back, great mouth and whiskers long as a Chinese mandarin's beard. Some of the people blamed the fish for the evil that had come on the village and the rector was called for. The sea went down and at noon the fish was stranded in a shallow pool of water along with flotsam from the storm. One of the sailors who had spent time in Russia said the fish was a sturgeon and it had been blown off course by the Rage. That night the villagers built a fire on the quayside and roasted the giant fish. They all feasted on it — nearly three hundred people — and afterwards there was enough left for the dogs, the gulls and even some to feed the pigs.'

A pause, a moth the size of a table tennis bat fluttered down in death to the floor. 'Man, can you tell a tale!' said Fidel. And then, with a grin, added, 'You should have kids. Bouncing them up and down on your knee, telling them about dem Rages of yours. White-eyed they'd be!'

And then he was gone. Julie, we guessed, the girl with skin like silk and eyes of speckled green and brown. Bless our father of seven. Through gritted teeth we lit our mosquito coils in preparation for our monastic night ahead.

CHAPTER
7

ICON
FISH

'Certainly, there is something cosmic about steelhead,
like the way that they keep to the bowels of the ocean,
in the cold darkness, running deep to avoid seals,
killer whales, halibut and above all man.'

WHEN YOU'RE A KID, any fish is an icon fish and that's how it should be forever. They are all pearls of nature, all with their own personalities and points of loveliness. With age, though, you realise that some fish are different, some more equal than others. It's the way mankind regards them as though our destinies are entwined and we walk, or swim, together towards the future. These are the species that mean a million times more than their weight to the people who understand them and often live alongside them. This is certainly the case with the steelhead, the sea-run rainbow trout of North America.

Though I was with him quite a while, I could never quite tell if Big Bob was joking about anything or not. He had a way with him that I found quite inscrutable so that when he said the most outrageous things you had no idea of knowing if they were true or false. Take the cabin, way, way out in the British Columbian wilderness with its door and stairs smashed half to pieces. 'Where Pa died,' Big Bob said pointing to the platform above. 'The grizzly broke in, chased him into a corner and did for him up there. Helluva mess,' he said thoughtfully. I looked for a twinkle in his eye but there was none. 'You think you're tough, boy,' he continued (and I don't particularly) 'but do you think you could stand it here? At night,

wondering why that branch snapped sudden like. Dreaming of a big hot face at the window. How long could you stand that, boy? One night? Two? Pa was here years off and on. Always excited as a kid to come up for the steelhead hereabouts. Guess he was happy near to the minute he died, planning the next day. Tying a fly perhaps. God damn that bear.' He looked me eye to eye, steely, hard. Just like ten days later in his house in Prince Rupert when he showed me a grizzly stuffed and monumental in his hallway. It wasn't too savoury — one eye crazed, mites around its genitals and mange on the vast paws. 'That's him. That goddamn bear. After I found Pa I tracked it into the woods and did for the punk!'

'Bullshit.' I could have sworn I heard young brother Clint's voice coming from the living room. But Big B did not blanch and I still don't know the truth about his Pa but there's no bullshit about his knowledge of steelhead.

In any language there are icons and always have been. Centuries before Westerners arrived on the East Coast, the native Indians venerated these sea-living rainbow trout, running their rivers to spawn. The Indians carved them, painted them, were buried with them and Bob knew all this: beneath the bear beat a heart of gentleness.

Bob introduced me to the Run of the River, a genuinely great book by Canadian Mark Hume and read from it. 'The history of the ocean and the earth is written on the skin of a steelhead, etched in the scales. I pushed her back into the river so she could tell her story to the glaciers.' 'Kinda mystical,' Big Bob said when he put the book down, 'but he got it about right. It's all pretty much fundamental stuff, you know, steelhead fishing.'

Certainly, there is something cosmic about steelhead, like the way that they keep to the bowels of the ocean, in the cold darkness, running deep to avoid seals, killer whales, halibut and above all man. And then they return to a river like British Columbia's Kwinimass, so small, so clear that the fish can be seen and their lifestyle learned

about. 'Most times, you see pairs of fish,' Bob said. 'A male and a female together but times, too, single males push up river. A real grandmama could have three or four males along with her. But what you never see is a female alone. There's perhaps six hundred mature fish use this river in a year so you must look out for them. You see them run even the skinniest creeks by day and then, after spawning, they'll be drifting back down to the sea. In groups again or alone. It doesn't matter as long as they all get there, past the bears, the seals and all. If they can get back to the sea, they'll fatten up on the prawns and come back another two or even three times. Tough critters,' he drawled. 'Damn proud fish. You'll see. They sorta look you in the eye and growl at you. Clear off. Get out of my way. I reckon they're using worse words than that though.'

Bob was right. Four days on, right up where the Kwinimass grew truly tiny, in the shadows of a snow-capped mountain, we took a pair of fish, a big male and a female, in consecutive casts. It's easy to get carried away in an environment as pristine as this, with fish as wonderful as these but I seriously can never remember such fights on a fly rod before. It honestly was as though they could run to all four points of the compass at once and even when they'd stopped doing that, there was absolutely no tiring them, or at least not for an age longer than you'd expect from any other fish. Bob caught the desperation in my eye as I was playing the big, gold-dusted male. 'Got the strength of the sea in it, boy,' he said. 'He's here with a job to do and he's not for giving up on it now.' After the fish were returned, we watched both the male and the female join up again and run together along the neck of the pool and disappear strongly into the morning light, just as if I'd never crossed their paths in life. 'Kinda mystical,' Bob said again as the 'V's of the departing fish settled back once more into the serenity of the stream.

I'd not want you to think that there was anything about Bob that wasn't absolutely rock hard though. Back on his boat in the bay at

144

night, he'd drop cages overboard and catch crabs the size of hams. Half a dozen of these he'd eat with a steak cut from a bison. And it would all be washed down with as many cans of Bud as you could count. Truly, I'd rather have picked a fight with Desperate Dan.

The police came out to check him whilst we were on the boat one evening. Five of them, pistol carrying, looking very mean. You see, Big Bob didn't have a licence for steelhead guiding and what were we all doing there then? 'Firstly,' he growled, 'don't any of you damn boys even think of setting foot on this boat without a warrant. Which you haven't got. And secondly, I don't ever guide for steelhead because I don't make money out of steelhead. What I do is bring friends to see steelhead so they can appreciate the finest fish that swims. Perhaps write about them. Paint them. Photograph them. Whatever. Just spread the goddamn message. Tell the frigging world. Any argument with that, eh, boys?'

Not that rainbows have to be mariners to be wonderfully beautiful. The very best of them I've found anywhere in the world have been living in New Zealand's North Island in and around Lake Taupo. I don't quite know how the river systems work there and I was totally confused about which were running in and which were running out but it didn't really matter with Ken around. Small, wiry and very antipodean, I think Ken was initially (and rightly) sceptical of my abilities but once he saw I could catch some fish on the dry fly — and he wouldn't allow anything else — he began to mellow. Mind you, it was a while before he showed me anything extraordinary. Each morning he picked me up and drove me off into the wilds to explore one crystal stream after another. They really were little nuggets of paradise, even those Ken complained of over-fishing and I supposed

the trout were kind of twitchy. But then again, what trout anywhere in the world wouldn't be a little wary in such gin water, on such bright days when the finest of leaders must have stood out above them like a hawser rope? I could see why Ken insisted on dry fly because it was heart stopping to see such perfect fish coming so clearly to the fly once, twice or even three times before taking — or aborting at the very last moment. Sometimes the fish would smack the fly with the tail up a good foot out of the water so great was the power of their thrust upwards.

Ken and I always fished apart and he was always coy about the numbers he caught. I don't want you to think that statistics are important with me so I hardly paid this characteristic any attention whatsoever. What I couldn't help hearing, though, now and again on the wind was Ken's quiet voice. 'That's mine.' Just a whisper on the breeze. Sometimes a rustle in the leaves. But it was mesmerising somehow and little by little, I found myself subconsciously but actively listening for it. In the end, I couldn't help but want to watch and on the second — no the third — morning I put down my rod and walked up river to where I knew Ken was fishing. I just couldn't help it but I felt guilty somehow - an intruder in someway as I stood framed in the trees. I made no attempt to conceal myself but Ken didn't notice, so intent was he on his fishing. After five minutes he rose and missed a fish. Ten minutes on another trout sucked in his fly, the line went tight and his rod bent for two or perhaps three seconds before a rainbow boiled on the surface and volleyed off. 'That's mine,' Ken sang out softly. Over the next hour the same puzzling scenario took place on three occasions and I went back to my own fishing just a little mystified.

Lunch time and after our ceremonial beer, Ken settled down for his traditional snooze in the long grass. His breathing became deep and regular and I edged off to have a look at his fly. Well, nothing there: just a perfectly normal little sedge...until I noticed the hook was snipped off beneath the barb. Of course. How this made sense. Especially with a man of Ken's genius. How many trout does a man like Ken want to actually land? The deception becomes everything. Let the fish rest. Don't spook the fish. I watched Ken asleep and my heart warmed towards him. On the outside, a little rough perhaps, with a vocabulary you wouldn't necessarily want your grandmother to hear, but inside beat the heart of an angling gentleman. Soon, my clippers were at work on my own little olive.

'Mine, I think,' I muttered as a three pound rainbow cartwheeled at the end of my momentarily tight line, shook his head and then dropped back free but grumbling under the branches to his lie. Come evening, I was as vague on numbers as Ken had been. 'Just a great day, mate. I've had the greatest of days, believe me,' I said. He caught my eye, darted for my fly in its keeper and grinned hugely.

'You deserve something for that,' he said. 'Tomorrow morning, be ready at dawn, eh?'

There was a chill in the air and mist on the meadows. The sky was just beginning to show blue though and it would be a glorious sunrise. Ken pushed his pick-up even further through the scrub and

then walked me until the light was flowing freely into the day. We were tracing a stream just a flip of a cast wide and averaging six gin-clear feet deep. I guess we'd gone about a mile or more when upstream we could see a large willow straddling the water. From even where I stood, a good sixty or seventy yards away, I could see three logs suspended in the water beneath it. What, for pity's sake was I looking for? Why had Ken frozen like ice, shrunk into a shadow? Of course, you're bound to know the answer to this: the three logs were, in fact, rainbow trout of a magnitude I'd never even guessed at before. Of course in stew ponds, rainbows can be fattened up like baby piglets to twenty pounds or more but here, in the wild, fish like these feed on a natural larder of insects...

I don't know how long it took us to cover that short distance to the willow but I guess it was fifteen or twenty minutes at least, both of us using every conceivable piece of cover until we got to within a rod's

148

length. In the water, with the sun now upon it, you could see every detail of those three remarkable fish. I can't begin to describe their colouring, a dusted gold, slashes of red and fins as fine and as delicately speckled as a thrush's breast. The whites of their eyes as they rolled. The cream of their mouths as they sipped in a nymph. And, the very best of all, just every now and again, one of the three would break surface to sip in a fluttering moth.

'Oh, my God, Ken,' I gasped. 'Oh, my God. I can't... now I just can't think of trying to catch those fish. They're too much.'

'I knew you'd say that, mate. That's why I brought you. Just to see them, not to even try to catch them. We'd never hold one anyway, not on any fly gear, not so close to that tree. I've been watching them for the whole summer and just thought you'd appreciate a look.'

Appreciate a look! Appreciate a look? Ken, I thought, you've taught me something I will never forget and you've shown me something that will be with me for the rest of my life.

Funnily enough, I didn't fish again that particular journey to New Zealand for the next two or even three weeks or so until I'd reached a rather smart lodge right down on the South Island. My host was insistent that I should join his party the next morning in a helicopter to fish some wilderness streams but I really did fancy the home river, a majestic piece of water, running through stunning scenery. 'I thought I'd just wander up the lodge water. Take my time. Drink it all in,' I replied to his insistent invitations. 'Well, you can, of course, but it's pretty useless, all fished out you know.'

I stuck to my guns and spent a day in paradise. I walked some eight or ten miles and caught ten trout — all wild browns and all on a dry fly. Well, I say caught... but... well you know! I guess the largest was very close to ten pounds and the smallest not a great deal smaller. I didn't see a soul, not even a footprint. I watched deer and even a mountain tar, in the distance, spying me from a crag. It was simply my best day ever with a fly rod and back at the lodge I told them all

about it. 'Yup,' said my host. 'I told you it would be crap. All fished out. We've had eleven doubles!' And worse, three of those eleven doubles were residing in the lodge's freezer. Oh, Ken, how do you say anything to people like that?

I don't know where you stand on fish hatcheries. I admit that they're technological marvels but perhaps they shouldn't necessarily be seen as examples of progress. The existence of a hatchery all too often is a testimony to our failure to protect the rivers we were blessed with. Put simply, we haven't been able to save our natural fish and so we replace them annually with our own creations. Rivers, we are told, represent our veins of life, the providers of our water, much of our energy and the means of carrying away our industrial and domestic waste to the sea. What they don't do is wash away our sinful neglect. And that's why hatcheries so often stand between rivers barren or fish rich. On the upside, hatcheries have had in part a nobler history and when refrigeration and steam-driven boats both appeared, fish populations around the globe would never be the same again.

Rainbow trout were introduced into New Zealand in 1883, the same year as browns made their way to the United States. Perhaps, though, the most unlikely and yet ultimately successful and hard-won introduction was that of trout to the Himalayas, to Kashmir in particular. The first batch of ten thousand trout eggs arrived from England in 1899, courtesy of the Duke of Bedford. In return, the Maharajah of Kashmir presented Sir Adelbert Talbert, the British Resident at Srinagar with a magnificent stag head. It was all very fine and the only down side was that every single one of the ten thousand eggs was found to have perished on route. Not deterred, the second shipment of trout eggs arrived in excellent condition, this time from Scotland, in the month of December, 1900. A certain J. S. Macdonald shepherded these fish as far as Kashmir and by the time that he arrived eighteen hundred of the eggs had hatched out into fry. A thousand of these were driven to a water fifteen or so miles from Srinagar whilst the rest were reared in the premises of a private carpet factory owner in the heart of the city. Things now were really buzzing: Frank Mitchell formed a private fishing club with twelve 'distinguished' British sportsmen with a subscription on £50 each. A large part of this money was used in establishing the first trout hatchery in 1901 and the records show that Gaffer Mir and Sodama Pandit were the first locals to be trained in fish culture shortly afterwards and paid five rupees a month by Mr. Mitchell. Of course, not everything could be expected to go smoothly and at least one of the stew ponds was destroyed by floods with the bay fish being washed into the adjoining Ara stream. Other intentional stockings took place and within just a few seasons it was found that the trout adapted stunningly to these virgin rivers. So much so that in 1906 a twelve and a half pound trout was presented by the state government to Lord Minto, then Viceroy of India. Certainly, by the 1920s, trout fishing was well established in Kashmir where it was praised by many as the very best in the world. Moreover, the Kashmir trout finglings formed the basis of stocking throughout the Himalayas, in Kulu, Himachal, Bhutan, Nepal and all along the northwest frontier.

It's a brave story of men with a vision for whom nothing was too much trouble or involved too much of their time. For men like Mitchell, mountains were simply there to be moved and the world was to bend to their will. Of course, playing God is a dangerous game and there are many such introductions of both flora and fauna that have proved to be less successful. As a glaring example, in many parts of Australia and the United States, most would class the appearance of carp as one of life's disasters and, in truth, in certain

conditions carp can become like locusts. They can over breed, cloud once crystal lakes and eat less bull-headed native species out of house and home. These become fish wanted dead or alive: they're netted, speared, shot with bow and arrow, fed to the pigs or spread to manure the land. And yet... and yet in other parts of the world carp are nothing less than fishy gods.

I never met Herman and now, sadly, he's dead I'm told but for a while he was the most sought after fish in Europe, perhaps. Herman was a carp — a fully scaled common carp — and I visited his home on a couple of dreary winter occasions. He lived in a puddle — a lake I suppose you'd have to call it — in the southeast of England and pretty horrible it was. As I remember, the place was ringed with chalets and there were streetlights so it was almost like a miniature town. On the island was a bar and above it loomed a dry ski slope. Worse, there were anglers everywhere even though in the foul weather their lines nearly froze to the rod rings and their breath hung in the still, cold air. What a crazy world and just imagine that giant fish edging over lines, under them, along them, testing every bite of food before he took it properly into his lips. How he must have wriggled close to the bank side at times or snuggled under the tree roots of the island for a little peace. Every now and again a bite indicator seemed half inclined to bleep, perhaps as his tail stirred the water and momentarily lifted a sleeping angler's tackle... anglers ringing the pool day and night, every second of every year. Never a dawning of peace for the fish, never a moment to drop guard. Was Herman ever able to greet the sun and drift like all carp do on the surface, fin hoisted, eyes positively rolling with laid-back delight? No, none of that for Herman. Did anyone even see him spawn, probably a hidden, hurried moment one early summer morning? Or was Herman in fact a her? Or perhaps even a trans-sexual, able to drift from one state to another as conditions dictated? A mixed up, stressful life, now perhaps gladly over. The anglers, I suspect, for the most part have probably gone now this weird stage is bereft of its great player.

Perhaps. That's always a word you've got to use when you're thinking about fish and it's possible that I've got it all wrong. Perhaps Herman was as happy as any other carp in the world, even those huge, unhurried zeppelins that laze their days away in Oolerts lake. It's every carp fishers dream to stumble on a lost lake, a water hidden and forgotten, holding huge and uncaught fish. Oolerts was manmade and the centrepiece of a formal estate but it was always a proof to me that nature can be moulded and designed into artificial scenes of beauty. In certain lights, from specific angles, Oolerts was as breathtaking as any other water I've ever seen. Waters... when you really, really get to know them, they mean different things to you, in their different moods and indeed in yours. Perhaps it's a freshness of a river that you want or the soul-stirring awe of a huge windswept loch. The gaiety of a highland stream, the seeping mystery of an estuary. Waters really do fuel your soul, fill your heart even, at times, water your tears.

Oolerts, as I've said, was special and so was its very biggest carp born, my researches suggest, in almost exactly the same year as I was myself. And so, over the decades this carp, a mirror with some huge scattered scales, was able to grow and grow in peace and serenity. I'd brushed with him during the late seventies and then again in the eighties without ever coming close to catching him I feel and it wasn't until 1997, when we were both well into our mid forties, that we were divided by a thread.

It was a warm, still morning with barely a hint of a breeze and the water was clearer than I'd ever seen it at Oolerts. It was so clear, in fact, it was as though it had been polished until it shone. I could see every swan mussel, every grain of sand, water beetles, water boatmen and certainly my own three pieces of hooked-up sweetcorn, coloured red, lying about thirty to thirty-five yards away from me.

I'd known for years that the big fish enjoyed this part of the lake at certain times of the day, partly I feel because of a spring bubbling into the water close by and perhaps just reducing the temperature a little. Anyway, as if by magic, it – let's start calling it she – appeared just on the right of my vision. I say as if by magic, because that's often the way with the monsters – they just somehow emerge as if spirited in from space. Oh, she was looking all right: you could tell by the way she held her body in mid water, by the way her fins were working with a very definite, easily readable intent. Then, over a space of fifteen or perhaps twenty minutes, she drifted imperceptibly forwards until she was hanging directly over the sweetcorn. Of course, I can't prove that she knew that it was beneath her just as I can't prove anything that I've said about fish in the entire course of this book. We might

nowadays have rubber fish singing to us, but that's not the dialogue we need to be sure, but I know, absolutely know that carp spent the next hour wondering whether to sip my bait in or not.

How do I know? Simply because I've been there so many times before, on a clear water faced with a large cunning fish who has had it in mind to take my bait. Sometimes a miracle occurs, all is pandemonium and I'm either ecstatic or cast down. But most of the time the fish wins the battle of wits, drifts away and I'm left feeling empty, drained. But which way would this showdown go now? What was that fish thinking? What on earth was she looking out for, what clues eventually gave my game away? The heat increased, sweat trickled down my back. The buzzing of the flies became near intolerable and wasps, coming down to drink, were continually crawling near my bare toes. I wanted to move, wipe my brow, scream even but I knew that the slightest flicker would betray me. She was watching. Perhaps it was my line in the water or even just a flare from my sunglasses but, after an hour or so, she shifted her bulk and drifted but with a definite purpose away towards the far tree fringe. That was it. The game was up and I'd lost it. That is how magnificent carp can be, how aware, how careful, capable of presenting a challenge as great as the wiliest wild trout anywhere. The question was whether I minded or not and the answer has to be no: it's a nice thought, somehow, this twin of mine, this great fish and I plodding together onwards into old age. And should I ever land it, what then? What on earth would you do when the moon is at your feet?

You can't have a chapter heading Icon Fish and ignore black bass — it just can't be done. The trouble is I've made it a rule only ever to write about what I know and even that can be tricky: how is it in late

night discussions I can never remember the best bits of shared reminiscences? And there aren't many reminiscences when it comes to Bailey and bass! In fact, I've only ever caught one small mouth and some fifty large mouths and the latter were from Spain anyway so I don't even know if they count in American eyes. The small mouth, though, was a major achievement in a minor sort of way, the best result of a most bizarre couple of weeks in upstate New York. Let me say a word about my companion here, Peter Smith. Perhaps you remember what I said earlier about not complaining…well, Peter wouldn't complain if his leg got bitten off. And cheery of spirits? Peter is positive to the point of maddening, even when the hire car springs a puncture at midnight, twenty miles north of Woodstock in a rainstorm out of Hitchcock. Drowned rats we undoubtedly were, but we made it back to our billet that night, the Smith spirit pulling us through.

Eva's guesthouse was our destination and she was lovely in a throwback to the fifties kind of way. Cutesy clothing and ash-blonde hair, she spoke with a beguiling hint of German woven into her adopted New Yorker English. To this day, I've never quite figured out what Peter and I were doing there. It was some sort of escape, I guess, for both of us with bass fishing as an excuse for us to fly the Atlantic. We'd come to the right place for quietness for Eva's truly was an eddy in life, so far out of reality you would never have guessed she was only four hours from JFK by road, the last ten miles along dirt track that we never quite sorted out, especially once darkness had fallen. Soon, though, we contented ourselves with Eva after nightfall. Why roam when you've found a haven from the storm? Eva madea breakfast of ten thousand calories or more and heaven help you if you didn't eat up your skyscrapers of pancakes. She had a little stream running through her garden where a pristine brook trout lived and a pond so full of frogs and newts you couldn't see watery space between them. Sitting on Eva's porch in the June night, listening to the symphony of secretive birds, bats, bears and lord knows what around us, Peter and I would look at each other and just snuggle down into our little oasis. If there were any problem whatsoever it was that everyone around us was quite mad. Eva swore she was worth six million dollars and the daughter of a German emperor – who I thought died in the 1920s and there was no way Eva was more than sixty! Her house, once grand, now listed so drunkenly that once you'd consumed those breakfast pancakes you could hardly claw your chair back to the table. Eva's tilt did make playing pool in the evening time easy, however, provided you could keep the white ball out of the down hill pockets.

Danny, was Eva's choice of guide and he we did find less benign. The night we arrived at Eva's, battered from twenty hours or more in the air and on the road, Danny insisted on a 5.00 am start for the bass we'd come so far to see. Damn and blast that bleary-eyed dawn, watching Danny's pickup burning the dust off the tracks, his face livid from consumption of pre-breakfast beers. 'Best get the night crawlers first,' he said. 'Don't trust them flies you boys got with you. The shop's not far.'

'How far?' said Peter, sharply for him.

'About five beers' worth,' replied Danny pulling a tab, trying to avoid a skunk already dead on the road. We crunched the animal and the open windowed cockpit filled with a stench so terrible you'd think all the sewers in the world had spewed.

Billy Bob's tackle shop was closed and from its faded stickers and grime washed windows looked to have been shut since catgut line was in fashion. Billy Joe's Emporium turned out to be only three cans away. We got there at seven thirty and we sat on the steps waiting for eight when, the notice said, Hank would be opening up. But Hank was clean out of night crawlers he said and told Danny that our flies looked alright to him so it was back along the eight beer road to the river next to Eva's garden.

That was the day that the weather cracked and the storm that had been lumbering eastwards finally arrived with a monsoon-like intensity. Eva's roof began to leak like a showerhead, the roads became a quagmire and the river swelled up brown. By now there were night crawlers up to our armpits and with them, Danny showed us how to catch binfuls of fully scaled common carp from the river in town. Beautiful, lean, golden fish they were indeed but not remotely resembling a bass. So, after two days, Danny recommended a stream ten beers away that should be running clear. Another dead skunk, two diners and four off licences later we pitched up at a bridge across a small, moderately clear river wherein lay a large shoal of brook trout in the three to five pound category. I thought Danny looked a little oddly at our evident excitement but contented himself with a Bud or two and a lads' mag while we thrashed the water to a foam. One of the 'brookies' eventually succumbed and after a short tussle, Peter beached a yellow, blotched fish with enormous fins and a mouth like a tunnel. There were hoots of laughter from two rednecks on the bridge. 'They'se suckers, boys. Trash fish. Suckers like you two I guess. There ain't been no bass in here twenty years or more. Tough shit or what!' We hit Danny awake and took to the road again, this time six beers to the east. There were no bass there either and back at Eva's we found the stream and the pond had coalesced and the house was a hopping carpet of frogs. 'When I get that damn money, I'll fix this old place up well and truly,' she hollered over the

water cascading into the strategically placed buckets. A lizard of lightning lashed out and the lights exploded with a flourish. 'And I'll get me a generator too.'

Danny did it at last. On a small, canalised river by one of the busiest highways in New York State, a two pound small-mouthed bass sipped in a gold head nymph amidst the thunder of the trucks. It fought like a ten pounder, looked like a whale and I knew instantly why bass are at the heart of American fishing. And, also, for what it's worth, one beer equals ten miles and eight hundred and ninety miles equals one bass! I have to add, in all fairness to Danny, that exactly a year on I went to Spain and caught those fifty big mouths. My two guides were highly skilled and their boat was state of the art. We caught fish from a crystal clear lake on flies, lures and rubber jugs. Everything they promised turned out to be true. It was perfect and professional and about a hundredth as much fun as life with Danny.

THE NEVER ENDING DREAM

'There is still a world beating with excitement, swimming with fish to stir the most sluggish of bloodstreams. Just as there are mountaineers, polar explorers, balloonists … so there remain piscatorial pioneers, men and women with dreams.'

YOU'D THINK THAT AIR TRAVEL, e-mails, satellite phones and the rest would have robbed the world of her secrets. You'd be wrong. You could say that logging, mining, irrigation and water storage schemes along with poaching and a million other examples of man's avaricious activities have blasted away the most extraordinary fish species for good. Again, not so. Yes, communities screened from the stage of history for millennia have been infiltrated and millions of people have changed their ways of life in a handful of years, a blink of the universal eye. To a degree. Settlements across the third — I prefer 'unknown' — world have often taken what they want from the West, adopting and adapting what might prove to be useful, frequently rejecting what is not. Peaked caps might appear to be an ugly excrescence from a cartoon but you'll find them around the globe simply because they serve such obvious purposes. Similarly, there aren't many kids who do not recognise a coke can. So, the world of fifty, even twenty years ago has vanished as completely as the age of the Incas but that doesn't mean it's not possible to find fabulous faces, witness time-honoured customs and wriggle beneath the veneer of uniformity. Remember under the broad brim of that blasted cap stare eyes that have seen a very different life to yours and a brain that takes many different slants on it too. There are still skies

of the brightest stars, hills cloaked in the darkest forests. Still the blackest of lakes, the bluest of rivers, still sights beyond our knowledge. There is still a world beating with excitement, swimming with fish to stir the most sluggish of bloodstreams. Just as there are mountaineers, polar explorers, balloonists...so there remain piscatorial pioneers, men and women with dreams. They would know what I mean: you close your eyes on the edge of sleep but only see the river of your desires. First, you just sense the scheme but now you're plotting the plan. Bed-bound but you're flying. An idea picked up from a magazine, a book, a documentary, the internet even. Calls to make, letters to write, faxes to send. You snap on the light to jot notes, your mind buzzing, your whole world spinning.

I'd like to recommend a book to you. Though long out of print, it's a regular feature at second-hand bookshops throughout Britain and the States at the least. *Game Fish of the World*, edited by Brian Vesey Fitzgerald and the redoubtable Francesca La Monte was published fifty-two years ago but most of what was revered then is talked of in hushed tones now. Just as we've learned a lot so we've forgotten a great deal too. One step forward, at least half a step back. It's arguable, for instance, that we know less about Goliath tiger fish in 2001 than Dr. Henry Gillet, one of the contributors to the book, did during World War Two. We know that they're the most terrifying freshwater predator on the planet but they live in the Congo basin which today is terrifying enough. My grandfather who died in 1935 knew more about North Sea tunny than any man alive presently...and now there's a whisper that they're returning to the Atlantic coast of Ireland. I pretend to know something about mahseer but what of the species when it gets into Tibet, into Burma, into the Euphrates where two hundred pounders were once regularly reported? And how about the char of Greenland's east coast, the brown trout of interior Iceland, the long-lost rhino fish of Africa, the serpentine eels in New Zealand, the goonch catfish of Nepal and

northern India, the pla buk of Thailand, the blue carp of China, the sea-run taimen of Kamchatka, the Atlantic salmon of the White Sea...it's enough to drive you crazy, to fill my own last years with plans ever-more manic.

And I'm brought to another book and author. Clive Gammon wrote his own book on travels, *I Know a Good Place*, years ago but he's still at it. I meet up with Clive here and there, a castle in Ireland most recently, and I recognise the total madness in his eyes. Clive is sixty or seventy, I don't know anything but that his physical age is absolutely beside the point. In his eyes you recognise the flame of the boy with a book at bedtime, the glow that will never be extinguished.

Occasionally in the past, an angler has been at the waterside when history had decided to shout itself out loud. You'll find such a moment on page 226 of *Game Fish of the World*. In September 1913, Sir Walter Egerton was fishing the Simmi, a small tributary of the River Rupunumi in the then named British Guyana. His quarry was arapaima — perhaps the world largest solely freshwater fish. Probably its least understood. To the natives of the Amazon basin they're better known as pirarucu — 'pira' for fish and 'urucu' referring to the bush bearing flaming red flowers — the exact colour of this creature's tail and lower body. So the colour is extraordinary, so too the shape — oddly cylindrical and cigar-shaped. And the size — probably reaching six hundred pounds, perhaps more. And it's remarkable biology. Since prehistoric times, the arapaima's swim bladder has evolved into a primitive lung leaving its gills as a rudimentary organ. This means, like you and me, this goliath fish has to breathe atmospheric oxygen to live. This gives them distinct advantages in low water: as flood waters recede, concentrations of

prey fish begin to gather in lakes and falling oxygen levels leave them lethargic and easy pickings for the energised arapaima. There's a down side: the fact that the arapaima has to surface every fifteen minutes or so to gulp down air makes it vulnerable to the watchful Amazonian with his sharp spear. Numbers have plummeted.

Hence few arapaima have been caught in nigh on eighty years since Sir Walter had his great afternoon. In two and a half hours seven arapaima weighing around two hundred pounds each were landed and bigger fish broke free. This was madness. Total chaos and there's probably been nothing like it since. Till now. This is not my story, though I've lived along the fringes of it so long names, places, weights and dates will be omitted until the noblest of captors breaks his own silence. This taster just goes to show that the most earth-breaking of adventures are still in our reach.

You'd never believe there could be so much rain in the skies over Brazil, you'd have thought that the gods had wrung the last of the moisture from the clouds draped solemnly above. But no, the storms keep coming, bending the world's giant trees, thrashing the river with raindrops, seemingly the size of pigeon eggs. Lizard-tongue lightning. Darkness at noon. The dug out canoe is taking in water so quickly a litre coke bottle is halved to provide two balers. And still it comes down and still the Amazon rises, challenging the forest, pushing its water deeper and deeper, linking one oily lagoon with the next. Squirrel monkeys fight and chatter in the trees. Macaws flash like lights against the black. Ringed kingfishers whistle over the water. Ever-cumbersome hoatzin birds jostle for the best overhanging branches. The noises of the forest melt into the sweep of the wind, bending the dense canopy above. Then they are drowned by the approaching grunts of thunder, even the macaws are eclipsed by the lightning that arcs across the inkpot sky.

The two Indians study the water intently, they've been paddling slowly for endless hours. The river here is narrow, perhaps thirty

yards wide, one of innumerable forks that twist this way and that through the vast forest. There's very little talking in the boat, an occasional cigarette is lit. There's no need for words, the only bonding needed is with the river. Both men are thinking the same thing, hoping that this strange English couple sitting in the boat behind them will see what they want to. Perhaps even catch the near impossible. If that were to happen, then their tips would be large, very large indeed. But that is not quite the point. Money's important, yes, but it's not everything. The two Indians want to see as well. They can only hope, half believe so they watch the water, willing something to happen. Can the sky grow darker? Can more rain fall? They all take it in turn to bale but the water level inside the boat continues to rise. And though they peer and peer again through the mist and the slanting rain they see nothing. It is as though the river is dead. Three days the Englishman and his wife insist upon going out but still they see nothing. They are mad. They must be mad. And very wet. The Indians look at each other. A barely perceptible shrug passes between them but the Englishman and his wife certainly don't notice: their eyes ache as they continue to scan the water.

In just an hour, the downpour has raised the level of the lagoon slightly, opening up a channel through the flooded forest, allowing the boat deeper into the jungle. Though none of the four people in the boat realise the significance of this, new water has opened up before them: the balance has changed. Soon, though, it will be dusk and the journey to the village is a long one. The Indians nod. Five more minutes. One of them is about to tell the Englishman this, on the point of taking his eyes off the water for the first time in twelve hours, when it happens. At the mouth of one of the inlets, ten yards from the boat, an immense shape breaks water, in an easy, silent, slow motion roll. The body is armour scaled, the fins paddle-like, immense. The fish must be over seven feet long. A monster. An arapaima, the rarest fish in the Amazonian basin, its sole home in

the world. The twin facts that it breaks the surface for air and that it keeps to the same patrol route for days on end have taken arapaima to the brink of extinction in all but the most remote areas, places like this. Indians and English can barely believe what they have seen: the driving rains, the hours in a boat, the endless journey to this lost place all count now for nothing. These are two of the very few Europeans for a century to see a living arapaima and tomorrow, because they know its whereabouts, they might just catch it. As I've told you, this is not my story so it's not for me to continue with it. What I can assure you is that there is absolutely, most definitely a tale that will one day grip the world.

Now, I want to tell you of our first three days with Ennisch, one of triumph and one of heartbreak.

The day was as blistering as it can be on the plains of eastern Mongolia as summer turns into autumn. A small group of us including me, Johnny and the Professor left the camp and walked across the endless flat flood plain of the Onon river for more than three hours, covering well over ten miles in the boiling heat. Ennisch led the way over terrain which was wild and marshy and we frequently found ourselves stumbling through swamp grass, in stale water up to our knees. Nor were the flies there any too welcoming either. We began to hate him. But, eventually, just as he had said, we came to a great lagoon formed from an oxbow lake, created by the river years ago. The water was crystal clear and rich in weed. Everywhere around the margins there were shoal fish, creatures almost identical to European bream and roach. We tried rubber fish, plugs and spinners for hours without a take. It was as though the water was completely devoid of any serious predator. Using scraps

from our lunch we tried to catch the little fish to use as live baits but again we failed.

Johnny and I had all but given up, sleeping in the long grass when there was a call from down the bank. The Professor was shouting for us unintelligibly. Our walk broke into a run when we saw his rod bent over and that he was playing a fish. We looked at each other. Was this at last it? The fabled Amur pike? A fish we'd come six thousand miles and eight days of travelling to see? We crowded round the Professor, peering into the water, shielding our eyes from the light. No. Gut wrenching disappointment for the fish we saw coming through the water towards us was a simple straightforward esox lucius. Perhaps six or seven pounds, the exact twin of any other jack pike we'd seen since our childhood. Then that fish broke surface, caught the sunlight and I tell you that we positively screamed. This was a leopard of a pike. With its tawny spots set on a cream background this was our first, cherished, beautiful Amur. For the first time but not for the last, we embraced Ennisch and the walk back to the camp that evening was like an escalator ride. We were on air. Our mission had at least halfway been accomplished.

The next day, we moved further east, deeper into a vast region of unexplored lakes and lagoons where the only transport could be by boat. This is a piece of the world virtually off the map. It's never been fished before by Westerners — of that Ennisch assured us. Mongolia is a deserted place even at its busiest and here there were no signs of any soul in the wilderness, no dwelling, track, livestock or any trace of man. The fishing was dramatically good. We had good taimen and at least six or seven smaller Amur, all about the size of that caught by the Professor the day before. We were beginning to think that the textbooks were all correct. Perhaps it is true that Amur just don't grow large and that ten pounds or so is their maximum weight. However, over supper that night, Ennisch insisted that this is not the case. 'One metre. One metre twenty. One metre fifty. All is possible.'

Johnny and I just listened, looking at each other and smiling. We didn't know Ennisch then. And anyway, none of this really mattered: we'd seen Amur anyway so a dream had been put to rest. And the wealth of the fish in this deserted place was simply amazing: red-tailed taimen, sturgeon, carp, outlandish trout species, all manner of whitefish, asp, zander...a piscatorial paradise is a term often over-worked but here we felt we'd found it. Even before IT happened.

Late the following morning Ennisch took us to a large lagoon some hundred yards or so from the Onon river itself. The depth was about six or seven feet and after a couple of small taimen and an Amur, again about six pounds, Ennisch insisted I try a new technique. He fished around in my bag and came up with a huge silver spoon, some eight inches long and weighing perhaps three or four ounces. He took off the plug I'd been using and attached this monstrosity. He told me to cast out, let the thing hit bottom and then work it very slowly through the silt so that it just kicked up puffs of mud as it went. I explained to him I would get snagged, that the spoon would just become a mud and weed encrusted lump of iron but he would have none of it and insisted I followed his instructions. For fifteen or twenty minutes I humoured him and at the end of each cast it would take a good thirty seconds to clean the spoon of all the debris. And then, on the fifth or perhaps sixth cast, the lure was suddenly and gently held up. I can't really describe the sensation – at the time I felt it had just moved into a patch of dense, soft weed.

This was obviously my undoing because I merely pulled as if to dislodge it rather than striking as if to set a hook.

In the best of fishing traditions, the weed pulled back! I couldn't for the life of me decide what I was attached to but it was obviously much too slow for a taimen and far heavier than any of the Amurs we'd tangled with so far. Catfish obviously sprang to my mind but after a couple of minutes it was quite apparent that this wasn't the case. None of those heart-stopping runs or that manic head belting down the line you associate with a big cat. No, this fish just kept slow and deep and plodded its own way around the lagoon. After ten minutes it was weakening and, piling on the pressure, I drew it into the shallows towards us. The sun was high, the water was clear and we could see everything: it was a crocodile of an Amur. The fish was at least thirty pounds and perhaps a lot more and we could see the spoon attached by the merest sliver of skin. You know what happens next: once the fish felt the water shallowing, its tail walked, shaking its head and that was the end of that. Still, another point proved, Amur do grow big.

Through the autumn of 1998, I began to regard Ennisch as much, much more than a guide to Johnny and I. I began to feel that with him little harm could come to us – a hunch soon to be pushed to its limits. He was a big man for a Mongolian, well over six feet tall and, I guess, around fifteen stone in weight. Unusual too, were his blonde hair and blue eyes intermingled with a strong Asiatic bone structure and dark skin. Guiding was not Ennisch's true profession, though he was very good at it: he was a trained geologist, unemployed since the collapse of a joint Mongolian/Czech enterprise a year before. 'I see no hope for Mongolia,' he used to say. 'No money. No jobs. Just alcohol. The people here want nothing more.' Losing his job and long term separation from his family didn't dampen his spirits unduly. Rather like a puppy, he walked us miles over the weeks and showed us amazing fishing. Each day he'd light a fire, cook us a trout and then curl up in a ball and sleep through sunshine or snowstorm. Then we'd cough in his ear and he'd spring up, walk us back, drink a bottle of vodka, tell us a dozen Mongolian jokes of which we'd understand one and then, in mid party, he'd snuggle into a corner and snore loudly until breakfast the following day.

It was Ennisch who showed us the junction of the Agz river with the Onon, remote under towering cliffs. In a glorious burst of fishing, Johnny and I took two big taimen and had two monsters squabble over a lure. I had a hooked seven pounder, attacked by a whale of a fish on the retrieve and lost another of at least fifty pounds on a dead bait. These were all scarlet tailed taimen that inspired more whoops of delight. Ennisch slept throughout by his fire.

One night it had snowed much too deeply for us to leave the huts early the next day. Whilst we waited for the sun to complete a thaw, Ennisch spread a map of the country out for us on the table. 'There are three hundred rivers in Mongolia,' he said. 'I visit them in my former work. This is why I know everywhere there is.' He pointed out the Altai range in the west, the river system bisecting it. 'Here grayling of five kilograms.' He noticed Johnny's saucer eyes. 'Yes, true and perch the same. Five kilograms.' He showed us hill ranges, still oases for snow leopards and valleys where bears came daily to feed. He pointed out the regions of wild camel, of boar the size of mules, of a plain where there stood a fabled mountain of gold and the burial ground of Genghis Khan. He pointed out the places of the Shamans, the territory of the Tsaatans, the range of the Mongolian Yeti. Then he came to a lake as far east as it is possible to go before crossing the border with China. 'I'm here twelve years before,' he said, 'Searching for oil with an American team. The lake is like a sea and deep. It is always blue. Everywhere is desert but there are mountains far away, always covered in snow. It is a place where no-one goes apart from hunters of deer and bear. There are no villages, no herders, no traders. The hunters tell me there are

Amurs in the lake. Big Amurs. Thirty-five kilograms. Maybe more. These are the biggest Amurs in the world. I did not believe till I saw for myself. One day the jeep not start and I walked by the lake. There is taimens jumping — taimens eighty or ninety centimetres long and after them is a leaping Amur pike. This is a great fish. Monster shark and it catches taimen in air and goes away with it and I see the hunters are right all along. One day, John and Johnny, you make trip there with me. It is very hard country but we strong and we do it. It is necessary I think.' The sun had cleared the tracks, the ancient jeep was waiting and we left him curling up for sleep, blonde head lying on the map of his dreamland.

There were nearly no dreams left for any of us. On October 6th, we left the camp on the Onon to travel some forty odd mile to the airfield. We found a ferry across the River Balsch which augured well, especially as there was a ferryman too! Better still, our AN2 was waiting for us on a remote stretch of grassland next to nowhere in particular. There was a ruined building, designed once to be a control tower, the remains of a fuel dump and a throng of Mongolians. Whenever word gets out that a plane is Ulan Bataar bound, people materialise from nowhere. I've never liked this: Oleg Antonov designed his little seven hundred and sixty horse power bi-plane back in 1946 with a view to it carrying no more than twelve people along with two children and a minimum of luggage. This fact tends to be unknown or ignored around Mongolia and this particular day seventeen of us were trying to get aboard, along with a five hundred litre churn of milk brought by a despairing farmer. Ennisch intervened. A vigorous argument took place and the milk was removed very reluctantly by the farmer who was appeased to a degree by the production of boarding passes for a few of his chickens! We were warned of severe headwinds, so knowing that we were overloaded and that the plane was at least forty years old, I prepared for an edgy flight. Not that any of us really cared: we'd been so long in the wilds and we were so desperate for a hot bath that we'd have ridden to Ulan Bataar with the devil himself. The airstrip dog cocked its leg against the Antonov's front wheel, the engine spluttered into life and we were beckoned aboard. It was 12.45 pm: we could bank on being airborne till at least four.

The journey was as bad as feared. Just to look around the cabin made me nauseous. Sweating, I took off my fleece, puffed it into a ball and settled down to sleep, catching Ennisch's eye, itself half closed but winking in friendship. I let my thoughts take over, not difficult after such weeks. I drifted back in time to the mountains and the rivers we had explored, to days of blinding sun, of blizzards and wolf-howling nights. I relived the fish we'd seen, the discoveries we'd made. Through my sleep I felt us descending. I was elated and took out my journal to jot down the spirit of this last dream and of that lost lake of the giant Amurs. I looked through the window but with a shock saw none of the familiar U.B. landmarks, just a tapestry of mountains and ravines. I was also aware of rivulets of oil streaming the glass and a rainbow haze of fuel clouding my side of the plane. I was a seat back from the cockpit and could sense the urgent activity in there. The engine stopped, spluttered a second and died for ever.

'3.01 pm. So this is to be it then. Strange how the stomach freezes but there's still a smile on Ennisch's face. Johnny's too. Thumbs up. Old Oleg built this bugger to glide so there's hope if we can find a place flat enough. Funny but it's good to have quiet at last. The racket has gone. Just the wind in the wings. It's like being a bird. A huge goose. Young Peter is so brave and Ennisch has gone back to sleep. I can't feel my stomach at all now. Numbed out. But there's a burning, bursting feeling in my chest I've never had before. Strange how quick the mountains are coming up. Every second clearer and closer. 3.06. Shit. The wing my side is coming up. We'll cartwheel. God help ...'

173

He did. The plane levelled out yards from the brown plateau and we careered a quarter of a mile over the arid soil. Luggage showered around us and it sounded like a panel had fallen off the fuselage but we slowed, stopped and all of us burst into applause. Not one of us was hurt — I'd ripped a trouser leg and broken my watch and it sits to this day showing 3.06, the sixth of the month. Ennisch slept through the hours we awaited rescue whilst I thought of that churn, that extra weight. We'd have dropped like a stone. Ennisch saved us when we should have been dead and worse, we could so easily have been corpses covered in milk.

Perhaps subconsciously, all those years ago, I privately adopted the search for the most perfect fish because I knew it would be impossible to complete. I've never been so blind that I haven't always known that there is no such single special creature because, in their own different ways, all fish are perfect. So, if I ever needed the excuse for endless travel, I certainly stumbled upon it. I came out to Morocco both to pull this book together and to look for a tiny form of marble trout I'd heard whisper of in the Atlas Mountains. A few days searching was spent with my guide Mohammed, just looking for a river course not dried out, never mind holding fish. On the fourth day, however, we walked through the fantastically bleached hills to a gorge where we did find fish — not the marbled trout that I was looking for but a rare form of gypsy barbel. I was delighted, quite ecstatic and Mohammed evidently thought I was crazy. 'So much excitement over so small a fish.' Later when we were drinking herb tea in the room of a Berber woman he noticed my Rolex — a present I bought myself after my original watch had been destroyed in the air accident. He asked me how much it had cost and then whistled, shook his head and said, 'So much money over such a useless thing. Look here. My watch hasn't worked for a long time and I not miss it

at all.' I tried to tell him that the watch was more than a timepiece: every time I looked at it I remembered that day in Mongolia. When I said that every time I put on that watch I know I'm still alive, he knew that I was mad.

On the third night, just before reaching our village, a terrifying tramp approached us through the dusk, all eyes and beard and outstretched hand. I went to him and pressed a hundred Diram note into this hand and he left us, disappearing into the gloom of the olive groves. Here we go... 'So much money, John. Too much I think.' I thought to tell him about the tramp who'd terrified me as a child and that by passing on a few pounds I'd help lay a ghost but I knew he'd never buy that one. But it turned out I was wrong about Mohammed that he was listening to what I was saying.

That night we shook hands and parted at the bridge, agreeing to meet at sun up the next morning. It seemed that Mohammed knew of a lake with a special type of carp in it...'We might have to go some while, John. It's far into the mountains. We take what we need and we spend two nights in villages with good people. It's fun. We see great things and have big adventure.'

Mohammed winks at me. I think he's got it.

TROU   T

N THO   AND

FF